# Words on WATER

## Droplets of Wisdom from Rivers, Lakes, and Oceans

*Quotations & Reflections*

Curated by

**Matthew L. Moseley**

Foreword by Craig Childs

***Words on Water***

***Droplets of Wisdom from Rivers, Lakes, and Oceans***

Curated by Matthew L. Moseley
Foreword by Craig Childs
Afterword by Michael Fiebig
Research Editor: Fletcher Lucas
Interior Layout by Griffin Mill
Cover design by Michael Nicloy

Hardcover ISBN: 979-8-9913280-6-7
Paperback ISBN: 979-8-9913280-7-4

Published by CG Sports Publishing

AN IMPRINT OF

NICO 11 PUBLISHING & DESIGN
MUKWONAGO, WISCONSIN
MICHAEL NICLOY, PUBLISHER
www.nico11publishing.com

N11
Be well read.

Quantity order requests can be emailed to:
mike@nico11publishing.com

Printed in The United States of America

*Words on Water* is a proud supporter of American Rivers.

Also by Matthew L. Moseley

**Dear Dr. Thompson**

*Felony Murder, Hunter S. Thompson and the Last Gonzo Campaign*

**Ignition**

*Superior Communication Strategies for Creating Stronger Connections*

**Soul is Waterproof**

*Adventure Swimming and Stories of Water*

Dedicated to

Kristin Howse Moseley

*Our love. Our water.*

# Tabel of Contents

# Foreword
# Words on Water
by Craig Childs

When did you realize you were a mystic?

It happened when you tasted river water, when you kissed rain puddles.

It happened every time you recalled that we are on the only planet in the solar system with liquid water, not just ice or a gas.

Water is motion. It carries a kind of music, sculpting the land with notes and measures, filling a glass like a song. When it's not there, you can still listen to it. Walk along a dry desert wash and the crisp sound of your steps in gravel is brought to you by water. The echo of your voice in a cavernous canyon. The green of the lone cottonwood. The cloud in the sky. It is everywhere.

Find a place without water, I dare you.

In these pages, Matthew Moseley has gathered voices that, if you listen page by page and flutter them through your hands, you should be able to hear something like a creek flowing over pebbles. For a decade, Moseley scribbled quotes from writers as he came across them in his readings, jotting down reflections on water that picked up speed as others joined in and sent him passages.

In this book, you will find Mark Twain reading the face of a river like scripture, Robert Macfarlane reminding us that we ourselves are water bodies, Robin Wall Kimmerer calling water a verb, Lao Tzu using water's softness as power.

Some passages speak of reverence, others of warning. All of them point to something we often forget: Water is alive, and it lives through us. It holds our reflections, but it also holds our futures. Every river tells us where we've been, and every estuary hints at where we're going.

By the nature of three molecules, one hydrogen and two oxygens, this fluid element bonds seamlessly to itself, going back to being whole without a second thought. Combine the drops, pour them into pages, and shake them out of this book like rain.

May the words in these pages send you back to your own waters—those you've crossed, those you've lost, and those that will never stop waiting for you. Open the book anywhere and see what comes out. May the passages draw you closer to the world that sustains us, flowing through every cell, every canyon, every future.

Baja, Mexico, January, 2026

*Craig Childs is a best-selling writer, naturalist, and wilderness explorer who writes primarily about the American Southwest. He is the author of more than a dozen books, including,* The Secret Knowledge of Water, House of Rain, *and* The Wild Dark.

# Introduction

# For the Love of Water

By Matthew L. Moseley

There is something sacred about slipping into water. As an open water swimmer, I've found myself in the middle of lakes before sunrise, rivers that cut through canyons like liquid lightning, and oceans that speak in a language older than time. We are all born surrounded by it. Our bodies are a collection of small flowing rivers. We are *of* water.

***Words on Water*** is a celebration of this liquid soul—the rivers that shape landscapes, the lakes that reflect the sky, and the oceans that cradle our continents. This book is a collection of quotes, insights, and meditations from poets, philosophers, scientists, astronomers and swimmers, among others. The words are droplets of wisdom that remind us: water isn't just a resource, it's a teacher. It is a spirit. It is life itself, flowing forward yet always returning.

As these reflections illustrate, water has been a source of inspiration throughout the ages. From the Romantics to Tribes to musicians and artists, to priests, philosophers and mariners. It appears in the earliest known language of Sanskrit. Water is our one universal and uniting connection.

While this curation spans literary and cultural history, these quotes no doubt are only the shimmering surface of a vast ocean of writing on water. Few other subjects have provoked such wonder and fascination as are revealed in these pages.

My love affair with water runs long and deep. As a child, I swam in the bayous of Louisiana, in Lake Calhoun, Bayou Desiard, and Lake Pontchartrain. After moving to Colorado and marrying my wife, Kristin, a water rights attorney, our family began canoeing down the Colorado River through Canyonlands. We've been going down rivers ever since. Our son, Charlie, is now a river guide, and our daughter, Amelia, has traveled to Washington DC to lobby on behalf of rivers.

From those trips in the early 1990's, I began a lifetime of long-distance adventure swimming. From 25 miles on Lake Pontchartrain to 47 miles on the Colorado River through Canyonlands. A 40-mile swim on the Green River to a first ever swim of 24 miles from the island of Culebra to Fajardo, Puerto Rico. I've raced across Lake Tahoe with Kristin by my side in a kayak. I've swum around Key West, the Golfo Dulce in Costa Rica, the Sea of Galilee, and waters in between. I've felt and tasted water around the world.

I have always loved reading and books. Whenever I run across a *bon mot* or stirring passage about water, I try to capture it in the reporter's notebook I've carried with me for most of my adult life. I collected these reflections in a file called Words on Water.

It wasn't until Kristin had a brain aneurysm and surgery that I started curating the quotes in earnest as a distraction from all the distress. While she was in ICU for 21 days fighting for her life, revisiting and researching these little droplets of wisdom about water lifted my spirits and gave me hope.

Many friends and colleagues contributed quotes for ***Words on Water***. Mike Fiebig, the director of Southwest

River Protection Programs at American Rivers, provided an especially generous collection of quotations and wrote the Afterword.

As a communications strategist, storyteller, and adventure swimmer, I've witnessed firsthand how water connects communities and clarifies values. When we protect it, we're protecting our future. When we honor it, we're honoring the deepest part of ourselves, our very humanity. To ensure a viable future, we must strengthen our connection with water.

Indigenous cultures the world over have a deep reverence for water, often viewing it as a sacred entity and life source, not just a resource. Many Native American Tribes believe water has its own spirit, which humans have a responsibility to protect. There is a chapter of Tribal Words and Proverbs that emphasizes water's interconnectedness with all life, its spiritual significance, and the importance of treating it with respect and revelation.

***Words on Water*** is intended to be brought along on any adventure. Pack it in a river library in an ammo can on a rafting trip. Put it in your backpack, picnic basket or tackle box.

Open any page and read a quote aloud. Or imbibe in quiet contemplation. Drink up these words beside a stream. Carry it to the shore. Get sand between its pages. Quote from it on a high mountain top, where the rivulets of snowmelt turn into wondrous rivers, leading to magnificent oceans. You, too, can be a part of the story.

Let this book serve as a reminder of water's power and poetry. Above all, let it inspire you to listen to its song and act on its behalf. I consider myself an Ambassador for Water. I hope you will, too. Otherwise, even with all their power and glory, rivers, lakes and oceans have no voice.

Long May We Float,

Matthew L. Moseley

Las Abuelas, Getches Family Cabin, Magnolia Road, Boulder County, Colorado. January 2026

Chapter One

# Water *as* Life

The face of the water, in time, became a wonderful book–a book that was a dead language to the uneducated passenger, but which told its mind to me without reserve, delivering its most cherished secrets as clearly as it uttered them with a voice. And it was not a book to be read once and thrown aside, for it had a new story to tell everyday.

Mark Twain, *Two Ways of Seeing A River,* 1883

The air smelled like Bayou Teche when it's spring and the fish are spawning among the water hyacinths and the frogs are throbbing in the cattails and the flooded cypress.

James Lee Burke, *Creole Belle,* 2012

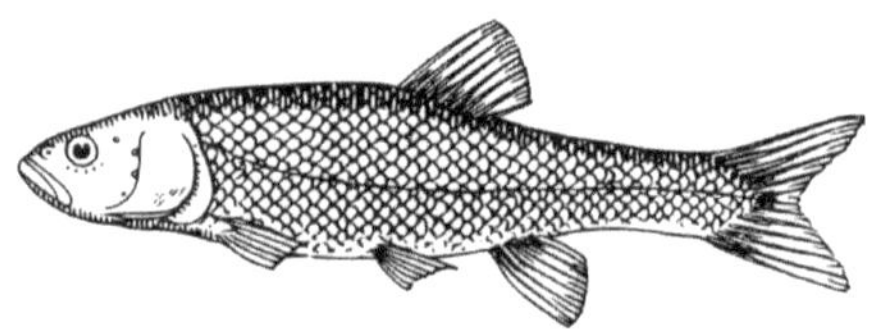

Run the rivers, breathe deep of that yet sweet and lucid air, sit quietly for a while and contemplate the precious stillness, that lovely, mysterious and awesome space.

Edward Abbey - 1976 speech in Montana,
Quoted in *High Country News,* 1976

Water is the driving force of all nature

Leonardo da Vinci, *Notebooks*, 1487

Keep your rivers flowing as they will, and you will continue to know the most important of all freedoms—the boundless scope of the human mind to contemplate wonders, and to begin to understand their meaning.

David Brower, Foreword to *Oregon Rivers*
by Larry Olson and John Daniel, 1997

If there is magic on this planet, it is contained in water.

Loren Eiseley, 1953

Empty your mind, be formless, shapeless, like water.
Be water, my friend.

Bruce Lee, *Longstreet*, 1971 television series

The sea, the great unifier, is man's only hope. Now, as never before, the old phrase has a literal meaning: we are all in the same boat.

Jacques Yves Cousteau, 2007

Meditation and water are wedded forever.

Herman Melville, *Moby Dick,* 1851

Thousands have lived without love, not one without water.

W. H. Auden, 1957

Water finds a way.

Captain Michael Feduccia, S/V Miss Cleo,
as told to the author

I have seen salmon swimming upstream to spawn even with their eyes pecked out. Even as they are dying, as their flesh is falling away from their spines, I have seen salmon fighting to protect their nests. I have seen them push up creeks so small that they rammed themselves across the gravel. I have seen them swim upstream with huge chunks bitten out of their bodies by bears. Salmon are incredibly driven to spawn. They will not give up. This gives me hope.

Kathleen Dean Moore and Jonathan W. Moore,
"The Gift of Salmon," *Discover* Magazine, 2003

It's clear to me that I will return here, as well as to other wilderness frontiers within me—whether next year or some time later—because I know that what the river says is what I need to hear: to know myself, to feel wild again, to confront my own limits and move beyond them into the untamed country on the other side. I will return here in spite of the river's name; but I will never return the same again, and that, after all, is most clearly what the river says.

Jeff Wallach, *What the River Says*, 1996

The good life on any river may... depend
on the perception of its music, and the
preservation of some music to perceive.

Aldo Leopold, *A Sand County Almanac*, 1949

Sail Forth-Steer for the deep waters only.
Reckless O soul, exploring.
I with thee and thou with me.
For we are bound where mariner has not yet dared go.
And we will risk the ship, ourselves, and all.

Walt Whitman, *Passage to India,* 1871

We must live with the River we have.
Not the River we want.

Becky Mitchell, Colorado River Commissioner,
*Salt Lake Tribune,* 2024

Nothing is softer or more flexible than water,
yet nothing can resist it.

Lao Tzu, 6th Century BC

You are not a drop in the ocean.
You are the ocean in a single drop.

Rumi, 13th Century Persian poet, *The Essential Rumi*

Water is life's matter and matrix, mother and medium.
There is no life without water.

Albert Szent-Gyorgyi, 1971

In one drop of water are found
all the secrets of all the oceans.

Kahlil Gibran, 1968

A river seems a magic thing. A magic, moving, living part
of the very earth itself.

Laura Gilpin, *The Rio Grande,* 1949

The cure for anything is salt water: sweat, tears or the sea.

Isak Dinesen, "The Deluge at Norderney,"
*Seven Gothic Tales*, 1934

I loved the rain as a child. I loved the sound of it on the leaves of trees and roofs and windowpanes and umbrellas and the feel of it on my face and bare legs. I loved the hiss of rubber tires on rainy streets and the flip-flop of windshield wipers. I loved the smell of wet grass and raincoats and shaggy coats of dogs.

A rainy day was a special day for me in a sense that no other kind of day was—a day when the ordinariness of things was suspended with ragged skies drifting to the color of pearl and dark streets turning to dark rivers of reflected light and even people transformed somehow as the rain drew them closer by giving them something to think about together, to take common shelter from, to complain of and joke about in ways that made them more like friends than it seemed to me they were on ordinary sunny days.

But more than anything, I think, I loved rain for the power it had to make indoors seem snugger and safer and a place to find refuge in from everything outdoors that was un-home, unsafe. I loved rain for making home seem home more deeply.

Frederick Buechner, *The Sacred Journey*, 1991

The River itself has no beginning or end. In its beginning, it is not yet the River; in its end, it is no longer the River. What we call the headwaters is only a selection from among the innumerable sources which flow together to compose it. At what point in its course does the Mississippi become what the Mississippi means?

T. S. Eliot, Introduction to Mark Twain's novel, *The Adventures of Huckleberry Finn*, 1950 edition.

The oaths of a woman
I inscribe on water

Sophocles, 406 BC

I'm an instant star. Just add water and stir.

David Bowie, 1976

People ask you why you live in Cuba and you say it is because you like it... you tell them the biggest reason you live in Cuba is the great deep blue river, three-quarters of a mile to a mile deep and sixty to eighty miles across... When the Gulf Stream is running well, is a dark blue and there are whirlpools along the edges.

Ernest Hemingway, *Holiday Magazine*, "The Great Blue River" 1949. Several years before publishing *Old Man and the Sea*.

We are a nation of rivers weaving across our countryside. They are some of our most important treasures and assets because our rivers include some of the cleanest drinking water that the world has ever seen... American Rivers has a tradition of being bipartisan, working with all political leaders. And we do that because rivers and water are something that unites all of us. All of us need clean drinking water, and that drinking water all comes from the same sources. So we see rivers and water as something that unites us as a country.

Tom Kiernan, President and CEO
of American Rivers, 2025

In the desert you celebrate nothing but water.

Michael Ondaatje, *The English Patient,* 1992

In the desert, the two primary elements are stone and water. Stone comes in abundance, exposed by weathering and a lack of vegetation. It is a canvas. Water crosses this stone with such rarity and ferocity that it tells all of its secrets in the shapes left behind.

Craig Childs, *The Desert Cries: A Season of Flash Floods in a Dry Land,* 2002

We are never far from the lilt and swirl of living water. Whether to fish or swim or paddle, or only to stand and gaze, to glance as we cross a bridge, all of us are drawn to rivers, all of us happily submit to their spell. We need their familiar mystery. We need their fluent lives interflowing with our own.

John Daniel, *Oregon Rivers,* 1997

He remembers how grandfather would say that the littlest streams, high on the mountain, small enough to dam with your hand, would eventually join the river, and that the river, though quick and violent, was but a drop in the eye of the great ocean that encircles all the lands of the worlds, and contains every dream everyone has ever dreamed.

Anthony Doerr, *Cloud Cuckoo Land*, 2021

The [Grand] Canyon and her dories embody and elusive riddle. It is a paradox rooted in the dream that many of us share of immersing ourselves so deeply, so inextricably, into a pocket of landscape, or a stretch of river - anything that seems to embody the wildness we have lost - that we may somehow take possession of those places and make them ours. Yet the truth, like an eddy, runs in the opposite direction. In the end, it is they that claim us. And we who belong to them.

Kevin Fedarko, *The Emerald Mile: The Epic Story of the Fastest Ride in History Through the Heart of the Grand Canyon,* 2013

At the end of the day on the water, I usually end up with at least a small pile of other people's trash, fishing line and old lures. I'm out there a lot and I always see a lot of trash along the banks and in the water and I always pick up what I can. I hate to see the negligence from fellow anglers… make sure you take care of your old line, lures and trash when you're out fishin' … and if you see someone else's stuff, pick it up and throw it away.

Billy Strings, Bluegrass virtuoso,
"Happy Earth Day, People," 2021

And you really live by the river? What a jolly life!" "By it and with it and on it and in it," said the Rat. . . . "It's my world, and I don't want any other. What it hasn't got is not worth having, and what it doesn't know is not worth knowing."

Kenneth Grahame, *The Wind in the Willows,* 1908

What we do on the Colorado River is being watched worldwide. It's one of the most managed rivers in the world, that supports a massive economy. And it's a bellwether for how highly managed, highly climate-susceptible rivers are going to deal with over-allocation and persistent drought. But for us in the conservation world and our partners in the Tribal world, the big question is: Is there room for the river itself?

Michael Fiebig, Director, Southwest River Protection,
American Rivers, *Rolling Stone*, 2024

## Ode to Watering

Over the earth, over grief,
water from your hand
for watering
and it seems as if
other water
falls in arcs,
not in cities for mouths,
for pots, but, while watering, the hose
brings hidden waters from the hidden fresh
heart spiraling up from the earth.

From there the trickle emerges,
evolving into water,
multiplied in drops,
aired out toward the lettuce's thirst.

From dust and plants,
a new aroma grows
with the water.
It's the wet scent of a green star,
it's the resurrection of freshness,
lost fragrance
of a lost heart
orphaned among the trees,
and water grows
like music in your hands:
with crystalline force,
you build a spear,
translucent:
it attacks, soaks and moves
in communication with the roots.

Pablo Neruda, *All the Odes*, 1973

Chapter Two

# **Water *and the* Infinite**

Something will have gone out of us as a people if we ever let the remaining wilderness be destroyed; if we permit the last virgin forests to be turned into comic books and plastic cigarette cases; if we drive the few remaining members of the wild species into zoos or to extinction; if we pollute the last clear air and dirty the last clean streams and push our paved roads through the last of the silence . . .

Wallace Stegner, *The Sound of Mountain Water: The Changing American West,* 1969

Preserving, protecting, and restoring our waters are tasks for many lifetimes, and sometimes the effort can seem overwhelming. But as long as we stay connected with all of the many, many blessings that water provides, and continue to keep that love in the forefront of our minds and hearts, as long as we remind ourselves to hope, then our stories will help connect others to water and encourage them to do what they can to help care for this beautiful Blue Marble world.

Wallace J. Nichols, *The Blue Mind: The Surprising Science That Shows How Being Near, In, On, or Under Water Can Make You Happier, Healthier, More Connected and Better at What You Do,* 2014

We have an unknown distance yet to run, an unknown river to explore. What falls there are, we know not; what rocks beset the channel, we know not; what walls ride over the river, we know not. Ah, well! we may conjecture many things.

John Wesley Powell, *Exploration of the Colorado River*
Journal entry on August 13, 1869

You don't need it, but will you take some advice from a Californian who's been around for a while? Cherish these rivers. Witness for them. Enjoy their unimprovable purpose as you sense it, and let those rivers that you never visit comfort you with the assurance that they are there, doing wonderfully what they have always done.

David Brower, Foreword to *Oregon Rivers*
by Larry Olson and John Daniel, 1997

Night and day the river flows. If time is the mind of space, the River is the soul of the desert. Brave boatmen come, they go, they die, the voyage flows on forever. We are all canyoneers. We are all passengers on this little mossy ship, this delicate dory sailing round the sun that humans call the earth. Joy, shipmates, joy.

Edward Abbey, *The Hidden Canyon – A River Journey,* 1999

Here in the United States we turn our rivers and streams into sewers and dumping grounds, we pollute the air, we destroy forests, and exterminate fishes, birds and mammals - not to speak of vulgarizing charming landscapes with hideous advertisements. But at last it looks as if our people were awakening. Many leading men, Americans and Canadians, are doing all they can for the Conservation movement.

Theodore Roosevelt, *Our Vanishing Wildlife*, 1908

You cannot see the Grand Canyon in one view, as if it were a changeless spectacle from which a curtain might be lifted, but to see it, you have to toil from month to month through its labyrinths.

John Wesley Powell, *Exploration of the Colorado River,* 1895

Water is nothing if not ingemination,
an encore to the tenacity of life.

Terry Tempest Williams, *When Women Were Birds,* 2009

People protect rivers they love, and love rivers they know.

Mike Fiebig, Director, Southwest River Protection Program, American Rivers

I gave my heart to the mountains the minute I stood beside this river with its spray in my face and watched it thunder into foam, smooth to green glass over sunken rocks, shatter to foam again. I was fascinated by how it sped by and yet was always there; its roar shook both the earth and me.

Wallace Stegner, *The Sound of Mountain Water: The Changing American West.* 1969 collection of essays

You don't need to see the ocean to feel its presence.
It moves through the air you breathe
and the water you drink.

Vicki Nichols Goldstein, Founder, Inland Ocean Coalition

For whatever we lose
(like a you or a me),
its always our self
We find in the sea.

E.E. Cummings
From Poem "maggie and milly and molly and may," 1958

Man - despite his artistic pretensions, his sophistication, and his many accomplishments - owes his existence to a six-inch layer of topsoil and the fact that it rains.

Paul Harvey, American Broadcaster,
*So God Made a Farmer,* 1978

But those who live by the myth, or pretend to, have never admitted that they live in a land of little rain and big consequences. Whether they are angrily protesting the setting-aside of areas of permanent wilderness, or trying to maneuver timber, oil, coal, mineral, or grazing lands away from the federal bureaus that protect them in the public interest, or speculating in oil-lease auctions or options in the water of federal reservoirs, they represent the survival of the gospel that left to its own devices would already have reduced a good part of the West to a desert as barren as Syria.

Wallace Stegner, *The Sound of Mountain Water: The Changing American West,* 1969 collection of essays

Till taught by pain, men know not water's worth.

Lord Byron, *Don Juan*, 1819

I would love to live like a river flows,
carried by the surprise of its own unfolding.

John O'Donohue, *Fluent*, 2004

Two ways the rivers leap down to different seas, and as they roll, grow deep and still, and their majestic presence, becomes a benefaction to the towns they visit.

Henry Wadsworth Longfellow, *The Golden Legend,* 1850

Water has always fought me, but I keep flowing down. Stopping would mean settling, and I don't settle for anything less than a life I can be proud of.

John Nichols, *The Milagro Beanfield War,* 1974

Have you also learned that secret from the river; that there is no such thing as time? That the river is everywhere at the same time, at the source and at the mouth, at the waterfall, at the ferry, at the current, in the ocean and in the mountains, everywhere and that the present only exists for it, not the shadow of the past nor the shadow of the future.

Hermann Hesse, *Siddhartha*, 1922

For many of us, water simply flows from a faucet, and we think little about it beyond this point of contact. We have lost a sense of respect for the wild river, for the complex workings of a wetland, for the intricate web of life that water supports.

Sandra Postel, *Last Oasis: Facing Water Scarcity*, 1997

You'll never miss the water 'til the well runs dry.

W.C. Handy, "Father of the Blues," 1915

Rivers are inherently interesting. They mold landscapes, create fertile deltas, provide trade routes, a source for food and water; a place to wash and play; civilizations emerged next to rivers in China, India, Europe, Africa and the Middle East. They sustain life and bring death and destruction. They are ferocious at times; gentle at times. They are placid and mean. They trigger conflict and delineate boundaries. Rivers are the stuff of metaphor and fable, painting and poetry. Rivers unite and divide—a thread that runs from source to exhausted release.

Edward Gargan, *The River's Tale*, 2002

A river seems a magic thing. A magic, moving, living part of the very earth itself—for it is from the soil, both from its depth and from its surface, that a river has its beginning.

Laura Gilpin, *The Rio Grande*, 1949

A boat may stay in water, but water should not stay in boat.
A spiritual aspirant may live in the world,
but the world should not live within him.

Ramakrishna, 1836-1886

I have never seen a river that I could not love. Moving water . . . has a fascinating vitality. It has power and grace and associations. It has a thousand colors and a thousand shapes, yet it follows laws so definite that the tiniest streamlet is an exact replica of a great river.

Roderick Haig-Brown, *A River Never Sleeps,* 1946

. . . the time has also come to identify and preserve free-flowing stretches of our great rivers before growth and development make the beauty of the unspoiled waterway a memory.

United States President Lyndon Johnson's Message on Natural Beauty, 1965

To stick your hands in a river is to feel the chords that bind the earth together.

Barry Lopez, *Drought*, 1994

The song of the river ends not at her banks but in the hearts of those who have loved her.

Buffalo Joe

A river, though, has so many things to say that it is hard to know what it says to each of us.

Norman Maclean, *A River Runs Through It*, 1976

We let a river shower its banks with a spirit that invades the people living there, and we protect that river, knowing that without its blessings the people have no source of soul.

Thomas Moore, *The Re-Enchantment of Everyday Life*, 1996

Can we afford clean water? Can we afford rivers and lakes and streams and oceans which continue to make possible life on this planet? Can we afford life itself? Those questions were never asked as we destroyed the waters of our nation, and they deserve no answers as we finally move to restore and renew them. These questions answer themselves.

Our planet is beset with a cancer which threatens our very existence and which will not respond to the kind of treatment that has been prescribed in the past. The cancer of water pollution was engendered by our abuse of our lakes, streams, rivers, and oceans; it has thrived on our half-hearted attempts to control it; and like any other disease, it can kill us.

We have ignored this cancer for so long that the romance of environmental concern is already fading in the shadow of the grim realities of lakes, rivers and bays where all forms of life have been smothered by untreated wastes, and oceans which no longer provide us with food.

Senator Ed Muskie of Maine,
arguing for the passage of the Clean Water Act in 1972

The river moves from land to water to land, in and out of organisms, reminding us what native peoples have never forgotten: that you cannot separate the land from the water, or the people from the land.

Lynn Noel, *Voyages: Canada's Heritage Rivers,* 1995

By such a river it is impossible to believe that one will ever be tired or cold. Every sense applauds it. Taste it, feel its chill on the teeth; it is purity absolute. Watch its racing current, its steady renewal of force; it is transient and eternal. And listen again to its sounds: get far enough away so that the noise of falling tons of water does not stuff the ears, and hear how much is going on underneath—a whole symphony of smaller sounds, hiss and splash and gurgle, the small talk of side channels, the whisper of blown and scattered spray gathering itself and beginning to flow again, secret and irresistible, among the wet rocks.

Wallace Stegner, *The Sound of Mountain Water: The Changing American West*, 1969

The wonders of the Grand Canyon cannot be adequately represented in symbols of speech, nor by speech itself. The resources of the graphic art are taxed beyond their powers in attempting to portray its features. Language and illustration combined must fail.

John Wesley Powell, *Exploration of the Colorado River,* 1895

We can choose to move like water
rather than be molded like clay.

Terry Tempest Williams
*When Women Were Birds,* 2013

The first river you paddle runs through the rest of your life. It bubbles up in pools and eddies to remind you who you are.

Lynn Noel, *Voyages: Canada's Heritage Rivers,* 1995

Wild rivers are earth's renegades, defying gravity, dancing to their own tunes, resisting the authority of humans, always chipping away, and eventually always winning.

Richard Bangs and Christian Kallen,
*Rivergods: Exploring the World's Great Rivers*, 1986

A river does not just happen; it has a beginning and an end. Its story is written in rich earth, in ice, and in water-carved stone, and its story as the lifeblood of the land is filled with color, music and thunder.

Andy Russell, *The Life of a River*, 1987

Who hears the rippling of rivers
will not utterly despair of anything.

Henry David Thoreau, *Thoreau's Journal*, 1841

... I shall now confess to you that none of those three trout had to be beheaded, or folded double, to fit their casket. What was big was not the trout, but the chance. What was full was not my creel, but my memory.

Aldo Leopold, *A Sand County Almanac*, 1949

The ocean unites us no matter where we stand on Earth. We are all inland, and we are all coastal.

Vicki Nichols Goldstein, Founder, Inland Ocean Coalition

Water, water, water...There is no shortage of water in the desert but exactly the right amount, a perfect ratio of water to rock. Of water to sand, insuring that wide, free, open, generous spacing among plants and animals, homes and towns and cities, which makes the arid West so different from any other part of the nation. There is no lack of water here, unless you try to establish a city where no city should be.

Edward Abbey, *Desert Solitaire,* 1968

The sea, once it casts its spell,
holds one in its net of wonder forever.

Jacques Yves Cousteau, 2007

Rivers run through our history and folklore, and link us as a people. They nourish and refresh us and provide a home for dazzling varieties of fish and wildlife and trees and plants of every sort. We are a nation rich in rivers.

Charles Kuralt, *On the Road With Charles Kuralt*, 1980

There are two easy ways to die in the desert–
thirst and drowning.

Craig Childs, *The Secret Knowledge of Water*, 2000

For me, it always comes back to the land... the rivers, mountains, and deserts, the absolute essential bedrock of our lives. This is the source of where my power lies... We are animal. We are Earth. We are water. We are a community of human beings living on this planet together.

Terry Tempest Williams, *The Progressive* Magazine, 2005

A river so clear and transparent that the bright stones suspended within its currents could be seen with the naked eye, glittering with the traces of an incontestable radiance whose depth and distance and truth lay beyond the reaches of any terrestrial imagination.

Kevin Fedarko, *The Emerald Mile: The Epic Story of the Fastest Ride in History Through the Heart of the Grand Canyon,* 2016

What does a river remember?

Colleen Miniuk, *The Current Flows* Exhibit, Santa Fe, New Mexico

There is no unhappiness like the misery of sighting land (and work) after a cheerful, careless voyage.

Mark Twain, Letter to his friend William Bowen in 1867

He thought his happiness was complete when, as he meandered aimlessly along, suddenly he stood by the edge of a full-fed river. Never in his life had he seen a river before—this sleek, sinuous, full-bodied animal, chasing and chuckling, gripping things with a gurgle and leaving them with a laugh, to fling itself on fresh playmates that shook themselves free, and were caught and held again.

All as a-shake and a-shiver—glints and gleams and sparkles, rustle and swirl, chatter and bubble. The Mole was bewitched, entranced, fascinated. By the side of the river he trotted as one trots, when very small, by the side of a man who holds one spellbound by exciting stories; and when tired at last, he sat on the bank, while the river still chattered on to him, a babbling procession of the best stories in the world, sent from the heart of the earth to be told at last to the insatiable sea.

Kenneth Grahame, *The Wind in the Willows,* 1908

Chapter Three

# Words *on* Swimming

As a matter of tradition, the rules (of open water) refer to a solo swim or relay where the swimmers are not assisted, supported, or touched by other swimmers or individuals on boats, kayaks, or paddle boards, do not wear wetsuits, and continue unassisted from start to finish. The tradition of channel rules began with Captain Matthew Webb's successful crossing of the English Channel in 1875.

Steven Munatones, former director of the World Open Water Swimming Association, *Open Water Swimming: Improved Performance for Swimmers and Triathletes*, 2011

I feel distance swimming is very important, not only as an exercise, but as a character builder. Once you've accomplished swimming a great distance, anything else in the world seems easy by comparison.

Annette Kellerman, first woman to attempt to swim the English Channel in 1905

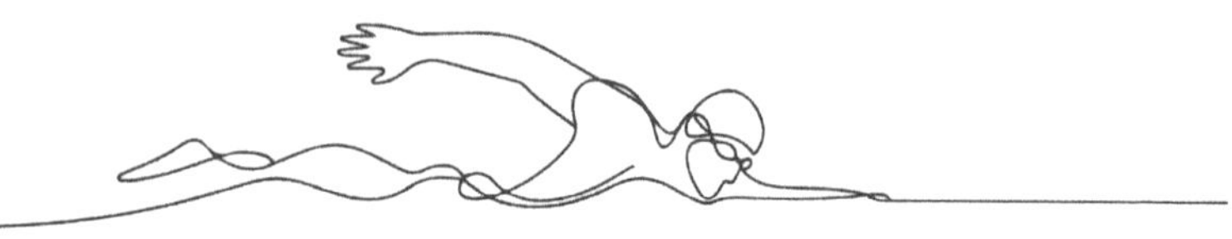

I've spent a lot of time before I take on a swim thinking about how to organize it, how I'm going to go about it, who's going to be on my crew, and how I'm going to train for it. When I actually do the swim, I'm really focused on making it across. Where am I in relationship to the boat? How fast am I going? Am I holding my pace, holding the straightest line, hitting the current or not? And I'm constantly adjusting my stroke to what the water is doing. I'm always monitoring. Sometimes I'm really sore or tired, and I have to focus on talking to myself just to keep going.

Or I'll stop to have some warm apple juice to keep my blood sugar up. And each swim is different. Going into Antarctica, there was constant concern about how cold the water was and going into hypothermia and dying.

Lynne Cox, the first person to swim across the Bering Straight in freezing waters in 1987

There are these two young fish swimming along and they happen to meet an older fish swimming the other way, who nods at them and says "Morning, boys. How's the water?" And the two young fish swim on for a bit, and then eventually one of them looks over at the other and goes "What the hell is water?"

David Foster Wallace, 2005 commencement speech at Kenyon College, "This Is Water"

He seemed to see, with a cartographer's eye, that string of swimming pools, that quasi subterranean stream that curved across the county.

John Cheever, *The Swimmer,* 1964

In the greatest city of the world in its time, it was more important to be able to swim than to be honest.

Alan Isles and John Pearn,
*Swimming and Survival: Two lessons from History*, 2013

Walking to the taffrail, I was in time to make out, on the very edge of a darkness thrown by a towering black mass like the very gateway of Erebus—yes, I was in time to catch an evanescent glimpse of my white hat left behind to mark the spot where the secret sharer of my cabin and of my thoughts, as though he were my second self, had lowered himself into the water to take his punishment: a free man, a proud swimmer striking out for a new destiny.

Joseph Conrad, *The Secret Sharer*, 1910

When someone appears in your life who strikes you as right for your support crew, bring 'em on. Look for qualities that Michael Fiebig mentions when describing water people–be it lake, ocean or river: Curious. Humble. Skilled. Hardy. Multifaceted. Prepared. Resourceful. Radically self-reliant. Jovial. Boat people get you where you want to go while minimizing friction instead of causing it. They deepen the experience because they exude a sense of quiet confidence. This lesson applies to life, as much as on the river. Find people who are your *thalweg*—those who keep you in the deepest strongest current.

Matthew L. Moseley, *Soul is Waterproof,* 2023

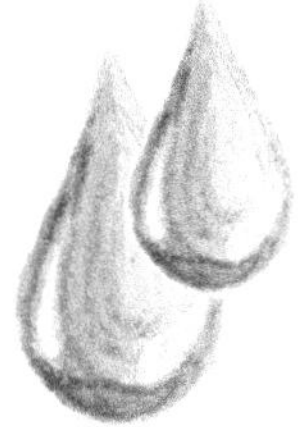

...the scourging of the surf made him red from the shoulders to the knees, and sent him on shore whipped by the sea into a single blush of the whole skin. He panted and shouted with pleasure among the breakers where he could not stand two minutes the blow of a roller that beat him off his feet and made him laugh and cry out in ecstasy.

Lord Swinburne, From I*n the Heart of the Sea: The Tragedy of the Whaleship Essex by Nathaniel Philbrick,* 2000

A man is not learned until he can read, write, and swim.

Plato, 360 BC

We are beginning to learn that our brains are hardwired to react positively to water and that being near it can calm and connect us, increase innovation and insight, and even heal what's broken.

Wallace J. Nichols, *The Blue Mind: The Surprising Science That Shows How Being Near, In, On, or Under Water Can Make You Happier, Healthier, More Connected and Better at What You Do,* 2014

There is an essential rightness about swimming, as about all such flowing as, so to speak, musical activities. And then there is the wonder of buoyancy, of being suspended in this thick, transparent medium that supports and embraces us. One can move in water, play with it, in a way that has no analogue in the air. One can explore its dynamics, its flow, this way and that; one can move one's hands like propellers or direct them like little rudders; one can become a little hydroplane or submarine, investigating the physics of flow with one's own body. And, beyond this, there is all the symbolism of swimming —its imaginative resonances, its mythic potentials.

Oliver Sacks, "Water Babies" *The New Yorker*, 1997

Why is almost every robust healthy boy with a robust healthy soul in him, at some time or other crazy to go to sea? Why upon your first voyage as a passenger, did you yourself feel such a mystical vibration, when first told that you and your ship were now out of sight of land? Why did the old Persians hold the sea holy? Why did the Greeks give it a separate deity, and own brother of Jove? Surely all this is not without meaning.

Herman Melville, *Moby Dick,* 1851

Learn fairly to swim, as I wish all men were taught to do in their youth; they would, on many occurrences, be the safer for having that skill, and on many more the happier, as freer from painful apprehension of danger, to say nothing of the enjoyment in so delightful and wholesome an exercise.

Soldiers particularly should, methinks, all be taught to swim; it might be of frequent use either in surprising an enemy, or saving themselves. And if I had now boys to educate, I should prefer those schools (other things being equal) where an opportunity was afforded for acquiring so advantageous an art, which once learnt is never forgotten.

Benjamin Franklin, *Memoirs of Benjamin Franklin,* 1791

Maybe I'm miserable and not having a ton of fun. I know if I'm in danger or conditions aren't good, they'll pull me out. But when it come to me or a personal choice, quitting is something I'm not allowed to do. Humans are conditioned to want to be comfortable. We want to be well fed and we want to be dry. So, when all of a sudden we find ourselves in these situations when we're not warm and we're not dry and we're not well fed and we're tired, the natural inclination is to want to stop and get out. I tell myself 'I'm tough. I'm strong. I can take it.' It's your mind that tells you it needs to quit. Not the body.

Sarah Thomas, first person to swim the English Channel four times consecutively. Personal interview with author, 2022

The water is your friend… You don't have to fight with water, just share the same spirit as the water, and it will help you move.

Alexandr Popov, Swimmer and winner of nine-time Olympic medalist and eleven world championships, the "Tsar of Freestyle," 1992

I feel most at home in the water. I disappear. That's where I belong.

Michael Phelps, interview with Donald McRae published in *The Guardian*, 2004

Water was something he loved, something he respected.
He understood its beauty and its dangers.
He talked about swimming as if it were a way of life.

Benjamin Alire Sáenz,
*Aristotle and Dante Discover the Secrets of the Universe*, 2012

And gentle winds and waters near
make music to the lonely ear.

Lord Byron, Hebrew Melodies, poem *It is the Hour*, 1815

The language of hydrological governance refers to rivers, streams and lakes as 'waterbodies'. To the forty thousand recognized waterbodies in England, Wales and Scotland should be added another 65 million or so—for every human is, of course, a waterbody. Water flows in and through us. Running, we are rivers. Seated, we are pools. Our brains and hearts are three-quarters water, our skin is two-thirds water; even our bones are watery. We were swimmers before we were walkers, slow-turning like breath-divers in the dark flotation tank of the womb.

Robert Macfarlane, *Is a River Alive?* 2025

You swam in a river of chance and coincidence.

You clung to the happiest accidents—
the rest you let float by.

David Wroblewski, *The Story of Edgar Sawtelle*, 2008

How could drops of water know themselves to be a river?
Yet the river flows on.

Antoine de Saint-Exupery, *Wind, Sand and Stars,* 1939

Being in the water for so long after swimming for 16-17 hours, you become one with the river. One with the water. You become immersed in it. You become a creature of the water. I feel like a fish. That I have as much right to be there as any other fish. There is something about endurance swimming that brings that out and also makes us good Ambassadors of the Water. We may tell its story so other people may care about it and want to save it.

Matthew Moseley, *Silent River* documentary, 2022

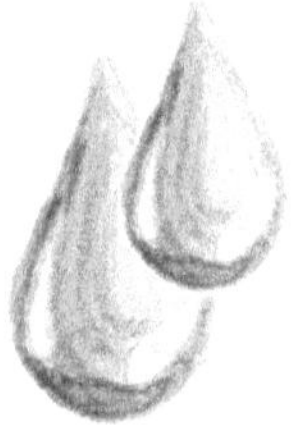

The sea-shore is a sort of neutral ground, a most advantageous point from which to contemplate the world....There is naked Nature, inhumanly sincere, wasting no thought on man, nibbling at the cliffy shore where gulls wheel amid the spray.

Henry David Thoreau, *Cape Cod,* 1866

A pool just isn't the same as the ocean.
It has no energy. No life.

Linda Gerber, *Death by Bikini,* 2008

Once more upon the waters! yet once more!
And the waves bound beneath me as a steed
That knows his ride

Lord Byron, *Childe Harold's Pilgrimage, Canto III*, 1812

Swimming is the writer's sport, because it is the sport most like writing. To swim, as to write, is to choose an intense state of socially acceptable aloneness. Swimming in the ocean is writing a novel, swimming in a pond is writing in a diary.

Hannah Yanagihara, "A Brisk Swim Across Martha's Vineyard," *New York Times,* 2016

I see a beautiful gigantic swimmer swimming
naked through the eddies of the sea,
His strikes out with courageous arms, he
urges himself with his legs,
I hate the swift-running eddies that would
dash him head foremost on the rocks.
What are you doing you ruffianly red-trickled waves?
Will you kill the courageous giant?
Steady and long he struggles,
He is baffled, bang'd, bruis'd, he holds out
while his strength holds out,
The slapping eddies are spotted with his
blood, they bear him away,
The beautiful lost swimmer.

Walt Whitman, *The Sleepers,* 1855

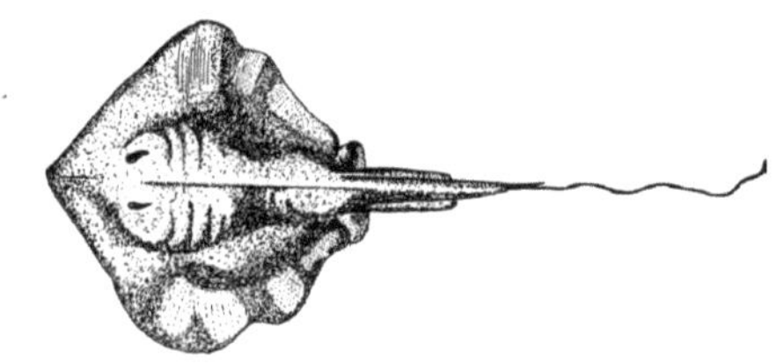

I delight in the sea and come out with a buoyancy of spirits I never feel on any other occasion. If I believed in the transmigration of souls, I should think I had been a merman in some former state of existence.

Lord Bryon, letter to his friend and publisher, John Murray, dated August 12, 1821, written from Ravenna, Italy, describing his daily routine and love for swimming.

### *Son of Water*

I was born from water.
From that blue abyss where fear dissolves
and the path is forged with every crawl,
every step, every stroke.
Water called to me when I needed it most,
when the weight of life drowned my dreams.
It didn't rescue me...
it taught me to swim toward hope.
In its embrace there are no judgments,
no borders, no names.
Water does not discriminate:
it welcomes the old, the young, the strong, the fragile.
We are all equal when we float. Its power is sacred.
It heals without asking, shapes without violence,
confronts you with your reflection
until you learn to love yourself.
The sea gave me purpose,
taught me that courage is not defeating the waves,
but embracing them.
That there is no defeat as long as you keep moving,
even if the currents push you back.
That's why I always return.
Because in every river, every lake, every ocean I touch,
I recognize the pulse of life itself.
There, in the liquid silence, I find God, myself, and the
meaning of existence.
I am a child of water, and as long as it exists,
I will keep swimming, for those who fear,
for those who dream,
for those who have not yet discovered
that water can also save them.

Joel Matos Ortiz, Guinness World Record Swimmer from Puerto Rico, 2025

If medicine be worthy of commendations, in respect of the nature in purging poisoned humors, drying away contagious diseases, and by this means adding longer date unto the life of man, well then may this Art of Swimming come within the number of other Sciences, which preserve the precious life of man, amidst the furious billows of the lawless waters, where neither riches nor friends, neither birth nor kin, neither liberal Sciences or other Arts, only itself excepted, can rid him from the danger of death, but it is also a necessary thing for every man to use, even in the pleasantest and securest time of his life especially: as the fittest thing to purge the skin from all external pollutants or uncleanliness whatsoever, as sweat and such like, as also it helps to temper the extreme heat of the body in the burning time of year.

Edward Digby, ***De Arte Natandi*** (***The Art of Swimming***)
First book ever published on swimming in 1587.

*Two of a series of woodcuts showing different swimming techniques.*

## On the Taste of Water

Closing my eyes and smacking my lips I can taste water from the Boulder Reservoir. I recall a deep chestnut, with notes of goose poop and a dumpster juice finish. Then again, on the Colorado River maybe it's more of a richly textured cappuccino, with a backwash of uranium tailings and a dash of Rocky Mountain gypsum. Swimming with the ghosts of Ernest Hemingway on Walloon Lake in Northern Michigan where he spent his summers and wrote, the shimmering early morning a reflection of the verdant forests coming alive after the winter frost, the water tastes like kissing a newly unearthed emerald. Maybe the Court of Master Sommeliers would consider including water connoisseurs? If such highly trained professionals can employ such lofty descriptive adjectives to give meaning to fermented grapes, surely the intriguing substance of water deserves as much.

Hours of swimming in the salty ocean can leave your tongue feeling like you've been licking the back of envelopes all day. The water of the Moab Boat Ramp evokes the taste of a bleached bone in the desert. Swimming in Destin and Pensacola I've picked up notes of fish scales and tarragon. Water from the Sea of Galilee brought to mind leavened bread. Lake Tahoe smacked of what I imagine chilled fine silk would taste like. The Red Sea felt like olive oil on the palette with afternotes of cardamon, rosemary, and crushed seashells. I've tasted iron and rust, rock and dust. A swimming hole in the Pacific Northwest offered a bouquet of forest floor. The water flowing from Rocky Mountain National Park into Lake Granby tastes evergreen, fresh, almost like fresh-cut summer grass.

But the best, purest water—like eating freshly fallen snow or splashing your face in a high mountain stream or plunging into the icy stillness of the deep Arctic Ocean—tastes exactly like nothing at all. The best water is clean and crystalline. The complete absence of flavor, what I imagine the Milky Way itself might taste like if you could reach your ladle into it. Just a little sip from inside the Big Dipper.

Matthew L. Moseley, *Soul is Waterproof,* 2023

Chapter Four

# Water *as* Spirit

I believe that water is the only drink for a wise man.

Henry David Thoreau, *Walden,* 1854

How you refill. Lying there. Something like happiness, just like water, pure and clear pouring in. So good you don't even welcome it, it runs through you in a bright stream, as if it has been there all along.

Peter Heller, *Dog Stars,* 2012

A lake carries you into recesses of feeling otherwise impenetrable.

William Wordsworth, *Guide to the Lakes*, 1810

Consider the subtleness of the sea; how its most dreaded creatures glide under water, unapparent for the most part, and treacherously hidden beneath the loveliest tints of azure..... Consider all this; and then turn to this green, gentle , and most docile earth; consider them both, the sea and the land; and do you not find a strange analogy to something in yourself?

Herman Melville, *Moby Dick,* 1851

Who looks upon a river in a meditative hour,
and is not reminded of the flux of all things?

Throw a stone into the stream, and the circles that
propagate themselves are the beautiful type of all influence.

Ralph Waldo Emerson, *Nature*, 1849

Shore where ever gayly dash the coming,
going, hurrying sea waves,

The mystic surf-beat of the sea,

The measur'd sea-surf beating on the sand,

The hurrying tumbling waves,
quick-broken crests, slapping,

The rocking in the sand, where they
rustle up hoarse and sibilant,

With rustle and hiss and boom and foam,

And rhythmic rasping of sands and waves,

With the surge for bass and
accompaniment low and hoarse,

And many a thump as of low bass drums.

Walt Whitman, *Of the Waters,* 1855

Live in the world like a waterfowl. The water clings to the bird, but the bird shakes it off. Live in the world like a mudfish. The fish lives in the mud, but its skin is always bright and shiny.

Ramakrishna, 1836-1886

And the pool was filled with water out of sunlight,
And the lotos rose, quietly, quietly,

The surface glittered out of heart of light,
And they were behind us, reflected in the pool.

Then a cloud passed, and the pool was empty.
Go, said the bird, for the leaves were full of children,
Hidden excitedly, containing laughter.

Go, go, go, said the bird:
human kind cannot bear very much reality.
Time past and time future what
might have been and what has been

Point to one end, which is always present.

T.S. Eliot, *Four Quartets 1: Burnt Norton,* 1943

Indeed the river is a perpetual gala,
and boasts each month a new ornament.

Ralph Waldo Emerson, Nature. 1849

Rivers must have been the guides which conducted the footsteps of the first travelers. They are the constant lure, when they flow by our doors, to distant enterprise and adventure, and, by a natural impulse, the dwellers on their banks will at length accompany their currents to the lowlands of the globe, or explore at their invitation the interior of continents.

Henry David Thoreau, *A Week on the Concord and Merrimack Rivers,* 1849

Rivers hardly ever run in a straight line.

Rivers are willing to take ten thousand meanders and enjoy every one and grow from every one. When they leave a meander, they are always more than when they entered it.

When rivers meet an obstacle, they do not try to run over it. They merely go around but they always get to the other side.

Rivers accept things as they are, conform to the shape they find the world in, yet nothing changes things more than rivers.

Rivers move even mountains in the sea. Rivers hardly ever are in a hurry yet is there anything more likely to reach the point it sets out for than a river?

James Dillet Freeman. *Rivers Hardly Ever: The Story of Unity,* 1954

Rivers are like people. We never destroy a river, for to do so would be to destroy ourselves.

Wade Davis, Magdalena, *River of Dreams,* 2020

The storms come and go, the waves crash overhead, the big fish eat the little fish, and I keep on paddling.

George R.R. Martin, Lord Varys in *A Song of Ice and Fire,* 1999

There's magic in the water that draws all men away from the land, that leads them over hills, down creeks and streams and rivers to the sea.

Herman Melville, *Moby Dick,* 1851

Before the land rose out of the ocean, and became dry land, chaos reigned; and between high and low water mark, where she is partially disrobed and rising, a sort of chaos reigns still, which only anomalous creatures can inhabit.

Henry David Thoreau, *Cape Cod,* 1866

We paddle our double craft into the current, ship paddles, lean back against the stern seats... We are indeed enjoying a very intimate relation with the river: only a layer of fabric between our bodies and the water. I let my arm dangle over the side and trail my hand in the flow. Something dreamlike and remembered, that sensation called deja-vu – when was I here before? A moment of groping back through the maze, following the thread of a unique emotion, and then I discover the beginning. I am fulfilling at last a dream of childhood and one as powerful as the erotic dreams of adolescence—floating down the river. Mark Twain, Major Powell every man that has ever put forth on flowing water knows what I mean.

Edward Abbey, *Desert Solitaire: A Season in the Wilderness,* 1968

What I think is interesting, or really challenging, is that I've been working on telling the story (of the Colorado River) for over a decade. I did a film a decade ago about shortage. And we are still talking about it. Nobody is getting it. I'm afraid the only way people will get that this shortage is happening is when the taps stop running.

Peter McBride, National Geographic Photographer, *Silent River* documentary, 2022

Life in us is like the water in a river.

Henry David Thoreau, *Walden,* 1854

Out of water, I am nothing.

Duke Kahanamoku, 1910. Surfer, Swimmer.
Engraved on his statue at Waikiki Beach, Hawaii

River is time in water
as it came
still so it flows
yet never is the same.

Barten Holyday, *On the River*, 17th-century English author and clergyman, 1631

SOFTNESS

Water wears down the stone. Water finds its course.
Even when dammed, the reservoir seeks every weakness,
every opportunity.
Water always wins—not by force, but by softness,
by patience, by persistence.

Shane Schieffer, *The Tao of a River Guide,* 2025

The man who is swimming
against the stream knows the strength of it.

Woodrow Wilson, President of the United States, *The New Freedom,* collection of speeches from 1912 presidential campaign

A river is the most human and companionable of all inanimate things. It has a life, a character, a voice of its own, and is as full of good fellowship as a sugar-maple is of sap. It can talk in various tones, loud or low, and of many subjects grave and gay... For real company and friendship, there is nothing outside of the animal kingdom that is comparable to a river.

Henry Van Dyke,
*Little Rivers: A Book of Essays in Profitable Idleness*, 1895

And this our life, exempt from public haunt,
Finds tongues in trees, books in the running brooks,
Sermons in stones, and good in everything.

William Shakespeare, *As You Like It*, 1623

The care of rivers is not a question of rivers,
but of the human heart.

Tanako Shozo, Japanese politician and social activist
(1841-1913)

From its fountains
In the mountains,
Its rills and its gills;
Through moss and through brake,
It runs and it creeps
For awhile till it sleeps

In its own little Lake
And thence at departing
Awakening and starting
It runs through the reeds
And away it proceeds,
Through meadow and glade
In sun and in shade
And through the wood-shelter
Among crags in its flurry
Helter-skelter
Hurry-scurry

Robert Southey, *The Cataract of Lodore,* 1820

Dark brown is the river,
Golden is the sand.
It flows along for ever
With trees on either hand.
Green leaves a-floating,
Castles of the foam,
Boats of mine a-boating,
Where will all come home?
On goes the river
And out past the mill,
Away down the valley,
Away down the hill.
Away down the river,
A hundred miles or more,
Other little children
Shall bring my boats ashore.

Robert Louis Stevenson, *Where Go The Boats? In A Child's Garden of Verses and Underwoods*, 1885

I was born upon thy bank, river,
My blood flows in thy stream,
And thou meanderest forever,
At the bottom of my dream.

Henry David Thoreau, Journals, 1842

It would be far better simply to admit our spiritual poverty...When spirit becomes heavy, it turns to water... Therefore the way of the soul...leads to water."

Carl Jung, 1972

But I also know that in places, the river still runs deep, and though I've floated it in these places, it hasn't revealed itself in such obvious ways. I know that it might be months—years, even—before I understand what it has to teach me. I still need to give myself over to the flow and pattern and rhythm of it to learn its lessons and hear its messages. The river is inside me now, I know, and I need only wait and see where the current takes me, and what lies beneath it.

Jeff Wallach, *What the River Says,* 1996

Where can you match the mighty music of their names? —The Monongahela, the Colorado, the Rio Grande the Columbia, the Tennessee, the Hudson (Sweet Thames!); the Kennebec, the Rappahannock, the Delaware, the Penobscot, the Wabash, the Chesapeake, the Swannanoa, the Indian River, the Niagara (Sweet Afton!); the Saint Lawrence, the Susquehanna, the Tombigbee, the Nantahala, the French Broad, the Chattahoochee, the Arizona, and the Potomac (Father Tiber!)—these are a few of their princely names, these are a few of their great, proud, glittering names, fit for the immense and lonely land that they inhabit.

Thomas Wolfe, *Of Time and the River,* 1935

The creative force flows over the terrain of our psyches looking for the natural hollows, the arroyos, the channels that exist in us. We become its tributaries, its basins; we are its pools, ponds, streams, and sanctuaries. The wild creative force flows into whatever beds for it, those we are born with as well as those we dig with our own hands. We don't have to fill them, we only have to build them.

Clarissa Pinkola Estes, Ph.D., *Women Who Run With the Wolves: Myths and Stories of the Wild Woman Archetype,* 1992

The oceans are the planet's last great living wilderness, man's only remaining frontier on earth, and perhaps his last chance to produce himself a rational species.

John Cullney, *Wilderness Conservation* Magazine, 1990

We Floridians have always assumed an arrogant mastery over our natural environment. And we have always presumed ourselves capable of obliging the water that is all around us to behave itself.

And so we straightened out the Kissimmee River because we found its twists and turns inconvenient. We ditched and drained the Everglades because all that useless water offended progress. We gouged the mighty Apalachicola River to make a superhighway for barges that really didn't need one. We drowned the Ocklawaha for cross-state shipping that never arrived. We did it because we could.

Ron Cunningham, *Ocala Star Banner*, 2013

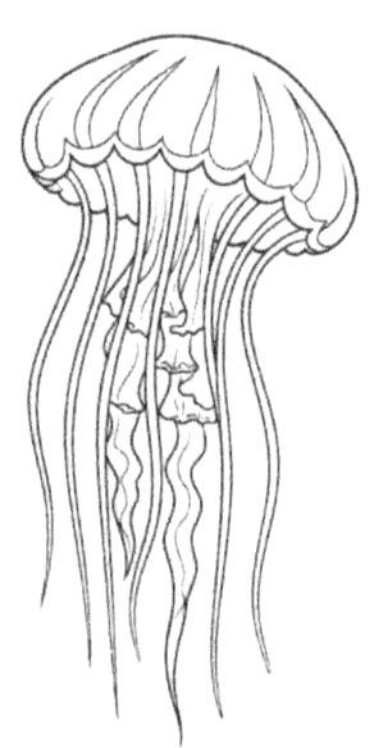

Even if you never have the chance to see or touch the ocean, the ocean touches you with every breath you take, every drop of water you drink, every bite you consume. Everyone, everywhere, is inextricably connected to and utterly dependent upon the existence of the sea.

Dr. Sylvia Earle, *The World Is Blue: How Our Fate and the Oceans Are One*, 2009

To trace the history of a river or a raindrop...is also to trace the history of the soul, the history of the mind descending and arising in the body. In both, we constantly seek and stumble upon divinity, which like feeding the lake, and the spring becoming a waterfall, feeds, spills, falls, and feeds itself all over again.

Gretel Ehrlich, Islands, *The Universe, Home*, 1991

Water is the best of all things.

Pindar c. 522 - c. 438 BC, *Olympian Odes*

Who owns Cross Creek? The redbirds, I think, more than I, for they will have their nests even in the face of delinquent mortgages. And after I am dead, who am childless, the human ownership of grove and field and hammock is hypothetical. But a long line of redbirds and whippoorwills and blue-jays and ground doves will descend from the present owners of nests in the orange trees, and their claim will be less subject to dispute than that of any human heirs.

Houses are individual and can be owned, like nests, and fought for. But what of the land? It seems to me that the Earth may be borrowed but not bought. It may be used, but not owned. It gives itself in response to love and tending, offers it seasonal flowering and fruiting. But we are tenants and not possessors, lovers and not masters. Cross Creek belongs to the wind and the rain, to the sun and the seasons, to the cosmic secrecy of seed, and beyond all, to time.

Marjorie Kinnan Rawlings, *Cross Creek,* 1942

Rivers are the primal highways of life. From the crack of time, they had borne men's dreams, and in their lovely rush to elsewhere, fed our wanderlust, mimicked our arteries, and charmed our imaginations in a way the static pond or vast and savage ocean never could.

Tom Robbins, *Fierce Invalids from Hot Climates*, 2000

When protected, rivers serve as visible symbols of the care we take as temporary inhabitants and full-time stewards of a living, profoundly beautiful heritage of nature.

Matt Rice, American Rivers, *Rivers at Risk,* 2023

We are under a multi-year drought and a lot of concerns about changing temperatures all over the globe, but in the West, it has impacts directly on water. One of the big challenges from a legal perspective is that it needs to be divided between people and nature, different states, and even different countries. Stream flows in the West are reliant on melt-off from mountain snowpack. The Colorado River starts in the headwaters of Colorado, but it goes all the way to Mexico—in its natural state. Due to drought and aridity, and the various places it gets diverted, it no longer gets to Mexico.

The biggest challenge to the river is overuse by humans.

Kristin Moseley, Water Rights Attorney,
*Silent River* documentary, 2022

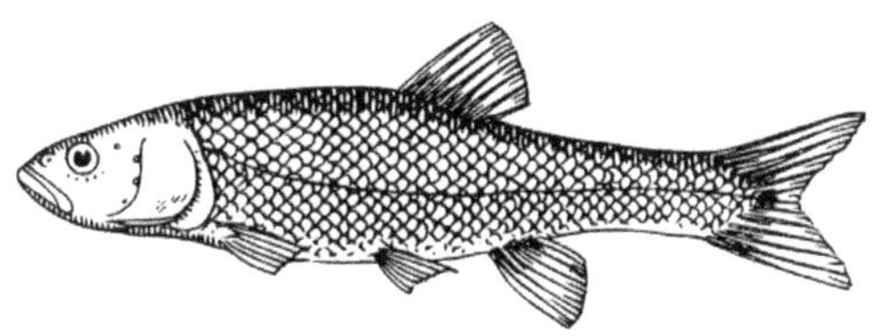

## To the River

Fair river! in thy bright, clear flow
Of crystal, wandering water,
Thou art an emblem of the glow
Of beauty—the unhidden heart—
The playful maziness of art
In old Alberto's daughter;

But when within thy wave she looks—
Which glistens then, and trembles—
Why, then, the prettiest of brooks
Her worshipper resembles;
For in my heart, as in thy stream,
Her image deeply lies—
His heart which trembles at the beam
Of her soul-searching eyes.

Edgar Allen Poe, 1829

Chapter Five

# Water *as* Teacher

That we live on land is, in the grander scheme of things, best regarded as an anomaly, even as eccentricity – albeit with sound evolutionary justification.

The story of life on Earth is, if we retain a true sense of proportion, a story of life at sea, and it is there that we must begin in order to really appreciate what water means to life.

Philip Ball, *Life's Matrix: A Biography of Water,* 2000

Water as a molecule (H2O) is found throughout the universe (in fact, it is the third most abundant molecule in the universe, after H2 and CO), but Earth is the only known world (and certainly the only world in our solar system) on which liquid water is currently found on the surface.

To me, this knowledge should make us all the more aware of the importance of maintaining the environment and climate that makes possible the oceans, lakes, and rivers that support Earth's diversity of life.

Jeffrey Bennett, Ph.D. in Astrophysics from the University of Colorado, Boulder; Author, and fellow swimmer, 2025

Water does not resist. Water flows.
When you plunge your hand into it, all you feel is a caress.

Water is not a solid wall, it will not stop you.

But water always goes where it wants to go,
and nothing in the end can stand against it.

Water is patient. Dripping water wears away a stone.

Remember that, my child. Remember you are half water.

If you can't go through an obstacle, go around it.
Water does.

Margaret Atwood, *The Penelopiad,* 2005

Of course, now I am too old to be much of a fisherman,
and now of course I usually fish the big waters alone,
although some friends think I shouldn't.

Like many fly fishermen in western Montana where the
summer days are almost Arctic in length, I often do not
start fishing until the cool of the evening. Then in the
Arctic half-light of the canyon, all existence fades to a being
with my soul and memories and the sounds of the
Big Blackfoot River and a four-count rhythm
and the hope that a fish will rise.

Eventually, all things merge into one, and a river runs
through it. The river was cut by the world's great flood and
runs over rocks from the basement of time. On some of
the rocks are timeless raindrops. Under the rocks are the
words, and some of the words are theirs.

I am haunted by waters.

Norman Maclean, *A River Runs Through It,* 1976

Wherever there is a channel for water,
there is a road for the canoe.

Henry David Thoreau, *The Main Woods,* 1864

My water law course is a thinly disguised course in trout fishing. When you trout fish, you need to think in terms of the whole watershed, and that's what you need to do with water law.

Charles Wilkinson, Author and Water Law Professor,
University of Colorado, 1991

In the world there is nothing more submissive and weak than water. Yet for attacking that which is hard and strong nothing can surpass it.

Lao-Tzu, *Tao Te Ching,* Chinese Philosopher
6th century BC

The river has taught me to listen;
you will learn from it, too.

The river knows everything;
one can learn everything from it.

Hermann Hesse, *Siddhartha,* 1922

Therefore the winds, piping to us in vain
As in revenge, have sucked up from the sea
Contagious fogs; which falling in the land
Hath every pelting river made so proud
That they have overborne their continents

William Shakespeare, *A Midsummer Night's Dream,* 1600

## HUMILITY

The River flows, not seeking credit or acclaim. It nourishes every canyon and bend, yet never holds anything for itself.

The Master rows with this same spirit—because she does not claim the River, the River carries her.

Shane Schieffer, *The Tao of a River Guide,* 2025

Imagine a limitless expanse of water: above and below, before and behind, right and left, everywhere there is water. In that water is placed a jar filled with water. There is water inside the jar and water outside, but the jar is still there. The 'I' is the jar.

Ramakrishna, 1836-1886

It is life, I think, to watch the water.
A man can learn so many things.

Nicholas Sparks, *The Notebook,* 1996

It is with rivers as it is with people: the greatest are not always the most agreeable nor the best to live with.

Henry Van Dyke, *Little Rivers, A Book of Essays in Profitable Idleness*, 1889

Children of a culture born in a water-rich environment, we have never really learned how important water is to us. We understand it, but we do not respect it.

William Ashworth, *Nor Any Drop to Drink,* 1982

It is said by the Eldar that in water there lives yet the echo of the Music of the Ainur more than in any substance that is in this Earth; and many of the Children of Ilúvatar hearken still unsated to the voices of the Sea, and yet know not for what they listen.

J.R.R. Tolkien, *The Silmarillion,* 1977

Half of me is filled with bursting words and half of me is painfully shy. I crave solitude yet also crave people. I want to pour life and love into everything yet also nurture my self-care and go gently. I want to live within the rush of primal, intuitive decision, yet also wish to sit and contemplate. This is the messiness of life—that we all carry multitudes, so must sit with the shifts. We are complicated creatures, and ultimately, the balance comes from this understanding. Be water. Flowing, flexible and soft. Subtly powerful and open. Wild and serene. Able to accept all changes, yet still led by the pull of steady tides. It is enough.

Victoria Erickson, *Edge of Wonder,* 2015

We ask a lot of water law. Since we depend on water for so much, it touches our deepest values. Besides its pervasive commercial importance, it is at the core of things we care the most about: health, sustenance, ecological integrity, and aesthetics. It even provides community identity and spiritual satisfaction. Is it possible to satisfy all these values? To design a legal system that provides stability and fairness? With so much at stake, water law presents unparalleled opportunities for analysis and creativity. It is an evolving field bristling with conflicts among people's most cherished values.

David Getches, *Water Law Nutshell*, 2008

…back when humans must have lived in almost continuous humility and awe, transfixed by the inescapable sense of just how small and unimportant they were—little more than Tadpole Shrimp or Spadefoot Toads, creatures unburdened by delusions that the world could be sculpted to suit their ambitions and needs.

Kevin Fedarko, *A Walk in the Park: The True Story of a Spectacular Misadventure in the Grand Canyon*, 2024

They both listened silently to the water, which to them was not just water, but the voice of life, the voice of Being, the voice of perpetual Becoming.

Hermann Hesse, *Siddhartha*, 1922

We forget that the water cycle and the life cycle are one.

Jacques Yves Cousteau, 2007

Ambho'si jīvanam loke

You (water) are the life in this world.

Sanskrit

I'm always happy when I'm surrounded by water.
I think I'm a mermaid or I was a mermaid.

The ocean makes me feel really small and it makes me put my whole life into perspective… it humbles you and makes you feel almost like you've been baptized.
I feel born again when I get out of the ocean.

Beyoncé, *Year of 4* documentary, 2011

The river of life is ever-flowing, and the Kumbh Mela serves as a reminder that all are united in the divine flow of existence.

YatraDham, on the Kumbh Mela,
the largest celebration of water on the planet

The ocean was the best place, of course. That was what she loved most. It was a feeling of freedom like no other, and yet a feeling of communion with all the other places and creatures the water touched.

Ann Brashares, 2012

The river called. The call is the thundering rumble of distant rapids, the intimate roar of white water . . . a primeval summons to primordial values.

John Craighead, *Naturalist* Magazine, 1965

Always be like water. Float in the times of pain or dance like waves along the wind which touches its surface.

Santosh Kalwar, *Quote Me Everyday*, 2010

The sea has never been friendly to man. At most it has been the accomplice of human restlessness.

Joseph Conrad, *The Mirror of the Sea*, 1906

My dear,
We are all made of water.
It's okay to rage.

Sometimes it's okay to rest.
To recede.

Sanober Khan, *A Thousand Flamingos,* 2020

Full fathom five thy father lies;
Of his bones are coral made;
Those are pearls that were his eyes:
Nothing of him that doth fade,
But doth suffer a sea-change
Into something rich and strange.
Sea-nymphs hourly ring his knell: Ding-dong
Hark! now I hear them—Ding-dong, bell.

William Shakespeare, *The Tempest,* 1611

Water seeks its own level. Look at them. The Tigris, the Euphrates, the Mississippi, the Amazon, the Yangtze. The world's great rivers. And every one of them finds its way to the ocean.

Alison McGhee, *All Rivers Flow to the Sea,* 2005

One cannot attain divine knowledge till one gets rid of pride. Water does not stay on the top of a mound; but into low land it flows in torrents from all sides.

Ramakrishna, 1836-1886

Water belongs to us all.

Nature did not make the sun one person's property, nor air, nor water, cool and clear.

Ovid, *The Metamorphoses of Ovid*, 8 AD

Be like water making its way through cracks. Do not be assertive, but adjust to the object, and you shall find a way around or through it.

If nothing within you stays rigid, outward things will disclose themselves.

Bruce Lee, *Longstreet*, 1971 television series

And I feel like the Queen of Water. I feel like water that transforms from a flowing river to a tranquil lake to a powerful waterfall to a freshwater spring to a meandering creek to a salty sea to raindrops gentle on your face to hard, stinging hail to frost on a mountaintop, and back to a river again.

Maria Virginia Farinango, *The Queen of Water*, 2012

Water is sufficient...the spirit moves over water.

Friedrich Nietzsche, *Ecce Homo*, 1908

You can lead a horse to water, but you can't
make him participate in synchronized diving.

Cuthbert Soup, *Another Whole Nother Story,* 2010

Where the waters do agree,
it is quite wonderful the relief they give.

Jane Austen, *Emma*, 1816

A glass of water has no value on its own, but the moment it quenches the thirst of an exhausted person, it turns more valuable than gold. Be a glass of water and quench the thirst of others. A glass of water doesn't need any fancy introduction to be hailed important, it doesn't need pomp and ceremony to be seen as significant, it doesn't need any fancy attire to appear appealing, all it needs to do is be there for the thirsty.

Abhijit Naskar, *Citizens of Peace:*
*Beyond the Savagery of Sovereignty,* 2019

Rivers' water rush by,
Nature's whispered lullaby,
Eternal, rivers lie.

Matthew L. Moseley, Poem

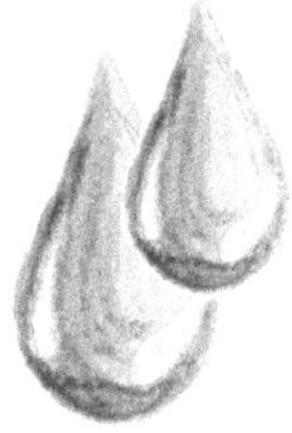

All the water that will ever be is right now.

*National Geographic*, Water: The Power, Promise, and Turmoil of North America's Fresh Water. 1993

America is a great story, and there is a river on every page. Let's remember that, and dedicate ourselves to the great work of restoring these rivers to health.

Charles Kuralt, *On the Road With Charles Kuralt,* 1980

Water links us to our neighbor in a way more profound and complex than any other.

John Thorson, Water rights lawyer and co-founder of the organization Dividing the Waters

Water is the most critical resource issue of our lifetime and our children's lifetime. The health of our waters is the principal measure of how we live on the land.

Luna Leopold, American hydrologist and geomorphologist, 2015

The earth, the air, the land, and the water are not an inheritance from our forefathers but on loan from our children. So, we have to handover to them at least as it was handed over to us.

Gandhi

Water is life and clean water means health.

Audrey Hepburn, actress, UNICEF spokesperson

When the well is dry, we'll know the worth of water.

Benjamin Franklin, *Poor Richard's Almanack,* 1732

So let the mind flow like water. Face life with a calm and quiet mind and everything in life will be calm and quiet.

Thich Thien-An, *Zen Philosopher, Zen Practice,* 1975

As man has within him a pool of blood wherein the lungs as he breathes expand and contract, so the body of the earth has its ocean, which also rises and falls every six hours with the breathing of the world…

Leonardo da Vinci, *Notebooks*, 1487

The highest good is like water.
Water gives life to ten thousand things and does not strive.
It flows in places men reject and so is like the Tao

Lao Tzu, *Tao de Ching*, 6th Century BC

You don't leave the water with the same perspective you entered it with.

Bonnie Tsui, *Why We Swim*, 2020

The health of our waters is the principal measure of how we live on the land.

Luna Leopold, American hydrologist and geomorphologist, 2015

Joys come from simple and natural things:
mists over meadows, sunlight on leaves,
the path of the moon over water.

Sigurd Olson, *Open Horizons*, 1969

There are many ways to salvation,
and one of them is to follow a river.

David Brower, Foreword to *Oregon Rivers*
by Larry Olson and John Daniel, 1997

Said the river: imagine everything you can imagine.
Then keep on going.

Mary Oliver, *White Pine*, "At the River Clarion,"
1996 poetry collection

Voices shape us like a river shapes her shores
along its course. We become what we listen to.

Colleen Miniuk, *So Said the River: Life, Loss, and Pie on the Colorado*, photographer, artist, storyteller,
Southwest River Council, American Rivers

We measure minutes. The river ignores millenniums.

Frank Waters, Sierra Club Bulletin, December 1965

I am keenly aware that there is something just now it seemed to flow in a rhythm around me and then to enter me - something which comes in a hushed inflowing. All of me is still and yet alert, ready to become part of this wave that laps the shore on which I sit.

Edith Warner, *In the Shadow of Los Alamos: Selected Writings of Edith Warner*, 2008

In the canyon itself the days flow through your consciousness as the river flows along its course… The current becomes the time on which you move. The river supplies in a sense supplants the need to measure time…there is no more liberating or healing experience. It penetrates to the very core of being, untangling knots and recreating the spirit.

Eliot Porter, *The Place No One Knew*, 1963

The flow of the river is ceaseless and its water is never the same. The bubbles that float in the pools, now vanishing, now forming, are not of long duration: So in the world of man and his dwellings... People die in the morning, they are born in the evening, like foam on the water.

Kamo no Chomei, *An Account of my Hut,* 1212

Time is a sort of river passing events, and strong is its current; No sooner is a thing brought to sight than it is swept by and another takes its place, and this too will be swept away.

Marcus Aurelius, *Meditations,*
Roman emperor and Stoic philosopher, 180 CE

I am the daughter of Earth and Water,
And the nursling of the Sky;
I pass through the pores of the ocean and shores,
I change, but I can never die.

Percy Bysshe Shelley, *The Cloud,* 1820

May what I do flow from me like a river,

No forcing and no holding back,

The way it is with children.

Rainer Maria Rilke, *Rilke's Book of Hours: Love Poems to God,* 1905

The Gay, the Straight, the Preacher,
The privileged, the homeless, the Teacher.
They all hear
The speaking of the Tree.
They hear the first and last of every Tree
Speak to humankind today.
Come to me, here beside the River.
Plant yourself beside the River.

Maya Angelou, *On the Pulse of Morning,*
recited at President Bill Clinton's inauguration, 1993

The Colorado is an outlaw. It belongs only to the ancient, eternal earth. As no other, it is savage and unpredictable of mood, peculiarly American in character.

Frank Waters, *The Colorado,* 1965

Rivers know this: There is no hurry.
We shall get there someday.

A. A. Milne, *Winnie the Pooh,* 1926

When I was young the waters sang
of being here before I am.

Greg Hobbs, Colorado Supreme Court Justice,
*Colorado Mother of Rivers*, 2005

When you work on water, you work on everything.

Mike Fiebig, Director, Southwest River
Protection Program, American Rivers

I choose to listen to the river for a while, thinking river thoughts, before joining the night and the stars.

Edward Abbey,
*Desert Solitaire: A Season in the Wilderness*, 1968

To have some parts flowing free again…with deer grazing on its banks…ducks and geese raising their young in the backwaters…eddies and twists and turns for canoeists…and fishing opportunities such as Lewis and Clark enjoyed…would be the finest possible tribute to the men of the Expedition, and a priceless gift for our children.

Stephen Ambrose, *Undaunted Courage*, 1996

When I saw what was going to happen to it [building Glen Canyon Dam to form Lake Powell], I was just in tears most of the time. That was the era of dam building, and they were going to build that damn dam no matter what. You take the blood out of the body, you die. You take the rivers out of our world, and we're no longer going to be here. We'd come along as some of the first river runners in 1950's here in this pristine Eden. It was just so astonishing. I couldn't get enough. I was always the first one up and the last one back. That experience made me who I am today. Glen Canyon is responsible for me. That canyon taught me how to touch things, how to feel things, how to listen for things, how to smell things. I wouldn't trade that for anything. I wouldn't trade it for the pain, the anger. The anger is still there. That's what keeps me alive.

Katie Lee, 1919-2017, actress, folk singer, and activist, called "The Desert Goddess of Glen Canyon," *What the River Knows* documentary, 2026

One major, overwhelming reason why we are running out of water is that we are killing the water we have.

William Ashworth, *Nor Any Drop to Drink,* 1982

Life originated in the sea, and about eighty percent of it is still there.

*Isaac Asimov's Book of Science and Nature Quotations,* 1990

High quality water is more than the dream of the conservationists, more than a political slogan; high quality water, in the right quantity at the right place at the right time, is essential to health, recreation, and economic growth. Of all our planet's activities--geological movements, the reproduction and decay of biota, and even the disruptive propensities of certain species (elephants and humans come to mind)—no force is greater than the hydrologic cycle.

Richard Bangs and Christian Kallen,
*Rivergods: Exploring the World's Great Rivers,* 1986

Men may dam it and say that they have made a lake, but it will still be a river. It will keep its nature and bide its time, like a caged animal alert for the slightest opening. In time, it will have its way; the dam, like the ancient cliffs, will be carried away piecemeal in the currents.

Wendell Berry, *The Unforeseen Wilderness,* 1972

The quality of water and the quality of life in all its infinite forms are critical parts of the overall, ongoing health of this planet of ours, not just here in the Amazon, but everywhere... The hardest part of any big project is to begin. We have begun. We are underway. We have a passion. We want to make a difference.

Sir Peter Blake, last journal entry before being murdered by pirates on the Amazon River, 2001

Any river is the summation of the whole valley. To think of it as nothing but water is to ignore the greater part.

Hal Borland, *This Hill, This Valley,* 1957

What makes a river so restful to people is that it doesn't have any doubt—it is sure to get where it is going, and it doesn't want to go anywhere else.

Hal Boyle, Pulitzer Prize-winning columnist for the Associated Press from the 1930s until his death in 1974

Sometimes luck is with you, and sometimes not, but the important thing is to take the dare. Those who climb mountains or raft rivers understand this.

David Brower, *Let the Mountains Talk, Let the Rivers Run: A Call to Those Who Would Save the Earth,* 1995

In a mucked up lovely river, I cast my little fly.
I look at that river and smell it and it makes me wanna cry.
Oh to clean our dirty planet, now there's a noble wish,
and I'm puttin my shoulder to the wheel 'cause
I wanna catch some fish.

Greg Brown, *Spring Wind from Dream Café*, 1992

We cannot make rivers whole
unless we wholly understand them.

Rob Brown, Wheeler School, Providence R.I.,
*Science Findings* Magazine, 2004

Estuaries are a happy land, rich in the continent itself, stirred by the forces of nature like the soup of a French chef; the home of myriad forms of life from bacteria and protozoans to grasses and mammals; the nursery, resting place, and refuge of countless things.

Stanley Cain, Speech "The Estuary a 'Happy' Land."
1963 Bays and Estuaries Conference.

Let the mountains talk, let the river run.
Once more, and forever.

David Brower, *Let the Mountains Talk, Let the Rivers Run: A Call to Those Who Would Save the Earth*, 1995

Little drops of water, little grains of sand,
make the mighty ocean, and the pleasant land.
So the little minutes, humble though they be,
make the mighty ages of eternity.

Julia Carney, *Little Things,* 1881

The Missouri is, perhaps, different in appearance and character from all other rivers in the world: there is a terror in its manner which is sensibly felt, the moment we enter its muddy waters from the Mississippi.

George Catlin, *Letters and Notes on the Manners, Customs, and Conditions of the North American Indians*, 1841

Water, water, everywhere, And all the boards did shrink;
Water, water, everywhere, Nor any drop to drink.

Samuel Taylor Coleridge,
*The Rime of the Ancient Mariner,* 1798

Ancient rock paintings remind us that there are no unclaimed lands, that people have always lived here. They are wayposts along the river journey to the interior of the mind and heart.

Lynn Noel, *Voyages: Canada's Heritage Rivers,* 1995

Next to blood relationships, which rule the valley, come water relationships. The arteries of ditches and bloodlines cut across each other in patterns of astounding complexity. Some families own properties on two or three of the valley's nine ditches.

Stanley Crawford, *Mayordomo: Chronicle of an Acequia in Northern New Mexico*, 1988

A river is the cosiest of friends.
You must love it and live with it before you can know it.

G.W. Curtis, *Lotus Eating: Hudson and Rhine,* 1877

Water is the creator and the destroyer…nothing we know could exist without it. Water has dark depths. It scoffs at man for his hubristic disregard of millions of years of carving and sustaining the cradle of civilization.

There would be no Prophet. No Bible. No Koran.
No Buddha or any belief or evolution without her grace.
No petroglyphs or poets.

Water is Namaste.
Water is Hallelujah.

Jennifer Julian Blow, Artistic Director, Co-Founder of the Bywater Museum of Unnatural History in New Orleans

Chapter Six

# **Water *as* Traveler**

In rivers, the water that you touch is the
last of what has passed and the first of that
which comes, so with time present.

Leonardo da Vinci, *Notebooks,* 1487

As the Master grew old and infirm,
he disciples begged him not to die.
Said the Master,
"If I did not go, how would you ever see?"
"What is it we fail to see when you are with us?" they
asked. But the Master would not say.
When the moment of his death was near, they said,
"What is it we will see when you are gone?"
With a twinkle in his eye, the Master said, "All I did was sit
on the riverbank handing out water.
After I'm gone, I trust you will notice the river."

Anthony de Mello, *One Minute Wisdo*m, 1988

Water, thou hast no taste, no color, no odor; canst not be
defined, art relished while ever mysterious.
Not necessary to life, but rather life itself, thou fillest us
with a gratification that exceeds the delight of the senses.

Antoine de Saint-Exupery, *Wind, Sand and Stars,* 1939

I understood when I was just a child that without water, everything dies. I didn't understand until much later that no one "owns" water. It might rise on your property, but it just passes through. You can use it, and abuse it, but it is not yours to own. It is part of the global commons, not "property" but part of our life support system.

Marc de Villiers, *Water,* 2001

Put on the river like a fleeing coat,
a garment of motion, tremendous, immortal.

James Dickey, *Deliverance*, novel, 1970

And see the rivers how they run.
Through woods and meads, in shade and sun,
Sometimes swift, sometimes slow,
Wave succeeding wave, they go,
A various journey to the keep,
like human life to endless sleep!

John Dyer, *Grongar Hill*, Welsh poet, 1726

To trace the history of a river, or a raindrop...is also to trace the history of the soul, the history of the mind descending and arising in the body. In both we constantly seek and stumble on divinity, which, like the cornice feeding the lake and the spring becoming a waterfall, feeds, spills, falls, and feeds itself over and over again.

Gretel Ehrlich, *Islands, The Universe, Home*, 1991

Water is the one substance from which the earth can conceal nothing; it sucks out its innermost secrets and brings them to our very lips.

Jean Giraudoux, *The Madwoman of Chaillot*, two-act play by French satirist, 1943

Water, like religion and ideology, has the power to move millions of people. Since the very birth of human civilization, people have moved to settle close to it. People move when there is too little of it. People move when there is too much of it. People journey down it. People write, sing and dance about it. People fight over it. And all people, everywhere and every day, need it.

Mikhail Gorbachev, Final leader of the Soviet Union, 6th World Water Forum, 2012

A whole river is a mountain country and hill country and flat country and swamp and delta country, is rock bottom and sand bottom and weed bottom and mud bottom, is blue, green clear, brown, wide, narrow, fast, slow, clean, and filthy water, is all the kinds of trees and grasses and all the breeds of animals and birds that men pertain and have ever pertained to its changing shores, is a thousand differing and not compatible things in between that point where enough of the highland drainlets have trickled together to form it, and that wide, flat, probably desolate place were it discharges itself into the salt of the sea.

John Graves, "Goodbye to a River" in *River Reflections,* 2002

A river is water in its loveliest form; rivers have life and sound and movement and infinity of variations; rivers are veins of the earth through which the life blood returns to the heart.

Roderick Haig-Brown, *A River Never Sleeps,*
1946 book on fly fishing

From the heart of the mighty mountains strong-souled for my fate I came, my far-drawn track to a nameless sea through a land without a name; I stayed not, I could not linger; patient, resistless, alone, I hewed the trail of my destiny deep in the hindering stone.

Sharlot Hall, *Song of the Colorado,* 1910

Ol' man river, dat ol' man river,
He must know 'sumpin, but don't say nothin',
He just keeps rollin', he keeps on rollin' along.

Oscar Hammerstein, "Ol' Man River," *Showboat*, 1927

You expected to be sad in the fall. Part of you dies each year when the leaves fell from the trees and their branches were bare against the wind and the cold, wintry light. But you knew there would always be the spring, as you knew the river would flow again after it was frozen. When the cold rains kept on and killed the spring, it was as though a young person had died for no reason.

Ernest Hermingway, *A Moveable Feast,* 1949

Between earth and earth's atmosphere, the amount of water remains constant; there is never a drop more, never a drop less. This is a story of circular infinity, of a planet birthing itself.

Linda Hogan, *Dwellings: A Spiritual History of the Living World,* 2007

A river is more than an amenity, it is a treasure.
It offers a necessity of life that must be rationed
among those who have power over it.

Justice Oliver Wendell Holmes,
New Jersey v. New York, et al., 283 U.S. 342, 1931

I've known rivers; I've known rivers ancient as the world
and older than the flow of human blood in human veins.
My soul has grown deep like the rivers.

Langston Hughes, *The Negro Speaks of Rivers,* 1921

Go softly by that river side,
Or when you would depart,
You'll find its every winding tied
And knotted round your heart.

Rudyard Kipling, *The Prairie,* 1896

If our salmon runs are not healthy, then our watersheds are not healthy—and if our watersheds are not healthy, then we have truly squandered our heritage and mortgaged our future.

Governor John Kitzhaber, Governor of Oregon, *A Tale of Two Rivers,* National Conference of Trout Unlimited, 2000

I started out thinking of America as highways and state lines. As I got to know it better, I began to think of it as rivers. Most of what I love about the country is a gift of the rivers. . . . America is a great story, and there is a river on every page of it.

Charles Kuralt, *On the Road With Charles Kuralt,* 1986

I sat there and forgot and forgot, until what remained was the river that went by and I who watched. On the river the heat mirages danced with each other and then they danced through each other and then they joined hands and danced around each other. Eventually the water joined the river, and there was only one of us. I believe it was the river.

Norman Maclean, *A River Runs Through It,* 1976

Water is H20, hydrogen two parts, oxygen
one, but there is also a third thing that makes
water and nobody knows what that is.

D.H. Lawrence, *Pansies,* 1926

Slowly it moves, and in mystic silence,
it draws me wondering,
Out through its shadowy portals to the ocean
where sails are blossoming.
Mary Stinton Leitch, *The River,* 1922

My soul is full of longing
For the secret of the Sea,
And the heart of the great ocean
Sends a thrilling pulse through me.

Henry Wadsworth Longfellow, *The Secret of the Sea,* 1850

Earth and sky, woods and fields, lakes and rivers, the mountain and the sea, are excellent schoolmasters, and teach some of us more than we can ever learn from books.

Sir John Lubbock, *The Use of Life*, 1894

If it's your Mississippi in dry time,
If it's your Uncle Sam when it's wet,
If it's your Mississippi in fly time,
In flood time it's your Mississippi yet.

Douglas Malloch, *Uncle Sam's River,* 1928

I often think about how the Colorado River is so much more than the clear water that comes out of all of our taps. There is the comforting sliding purr of an eddy and its glassy reflection during a calm dusk. There is the mud, where if put strategically is beneficial and could feed millions; when the Colorado was in flood, it flowed outside its banks and brought its well-traveled silty nutrient soils into the floodplain where the vast majority of the farmlands in the Imperial Valley of Southern California are located. There is the light off of the water. In monsoonal times, there is carving and voraciously changing events. In times of scarcity there is an overwhelming quiet. As it cycles through an annual hydraulic cycle each year, the Colorado is shirking to hide amid its arid surroundings.

Mike DeHoff, founder of the Returning Rapids Project, “Who is in Charge of the Mud?” University of New Mexico Natural Resources Law Journal, 2022

Wetlands have a poor public image. . . Yet they are among the earth's greatest natural assets. . . mankind's waterlogged wealth.

Edward Maltby, *Waterlogged Wealth,* 1986

There is an extreme beauty in the Ohio river…it appears deeply embedded in the wild forest scenery thro' which it flows. The whole stream is alive with small fresh-water turtle, who play on the surface of its clear water; while the most beautiful varieties of the butterfly tribe cross from one side to the other, from the slave-States to the free—their liberty at all events, not being interfered with, as, on the free side it would be thought absurd to catch what would not produce a cent: while on the slaves', their idleness and indifference to them are their security.

Captain Fredrick Marryat, *A Diary in America*, 1839

Swift or smooth, broad as the Hudson or narrow enough to scrape your gunwales, every river is a world of its own, unique in pattern and personality. Each mile on a river will take you further from home than a hundred miles on a road.

Bob Marshall, forester, conservationist, and co-founder of The Wilderness Society, 1933

Nothing alters a river as totally as a dam. A reservoir is the antithesis of a river—the essence of a river is that it flows, the essence of a reservoir is that it is still. A symbiotic relationship cannot exist when the essential character of one of the organisms is denied.

Patrick McCully, *Silenced Rivers*, 1996

The average person is two thirds river water and ought to have more sense about these things that he has shown. Obviously, a creature that is itself made mostly of rivers would do well to offer itself to the exaltation of rivers in good works and ceremonial acts of worship like fishing an contemplative floating in poetic watercraft like canoes. Rivers originally had all that they would ever need. They are the paragon of creation.

Tom McGuane & Joseph Barbato, *Heart of the Land: Essays on the Last Great Place*s, 1996

Men travel far to see a city, but few seem curious about a river. Every river has, nevertheless, its individuality, its great silent interest. Every river has, moreover, its influence over the people who pass their lives within sight of its waters.

H. S. Merriman, *The Sowers*, 1895

Rivers course through my dreams, rivers cold and fast, rivers well-known and rivers nameless, rivers that seem like ribbons of blue water twisting through wide valleys, narrow rivers folded in layers of darkening shadows, rivers that have eroded down deep into a mountain's belly, sculpted the land. Peeled back the planet's history exposing the texture of time itself.

Harry Middleton, *Rivers of Memory,* 1993

Sometimes, if you stand on the bottom rail of a bridge and lean over to watch the river slipping slowly away beneath you, you will suddenly know everything there is to be known.

A. A. Milne,
*Winne-the-Pooh and Piglet Build a House,* 1926

I wondered whether water is a mirror for our darker emotions as much as it is an engine for our happiness. Water quiets all the noise, all the distractions, and connects you to your own thoughts.

Wallace J. Nichols, *The Blue Mind: The Surprising Science That Shows How Being Near, In, On, or Under Water Can Make You Happier, Healthier, More Connected and Better at What You Do,* 2014

Rivers are magnets for the imagination, for conscious pondering and subconscious dreams, thrills and fears. People stare into the moving water, captivated, as they are when gazing into a fire. What is it that draws and holds us? The rivers' reflections of our lives and experiences are endless. The water calls up our own ambitions of flowing with ease, of navigating the unknown. Streams represent constant rebirth. The waters flow in, forever new, yet forever the same; they complete a journey from beginning to end, and then they embark on the journey again.

Tim Palmer, *Lifelines,* 2004

Rivers are roads that move and
carry us whither we wish to go.

Emerson Hough, *The Mississippi Bubble*, 1902

He who does not know his way to
the sea should take a river for his guide.

Plautus, *Poenulus* (or *The Carthaginian*),
in Act 3, Scene 3, line 14, 190 BC

Rivers are animate, in their way. They move. They breathe...To drown a river beneath its own impounded water, by damming, is to kill what was and settle for something else... It's a tragedy of diminishment for the whole planet, a loss of one more wild thing, leaving Earth just a little flatter and tamer and simpler and uglier than before.

David Quamman, *Grabbing the Loop,* 2012

There is no rushing a river. When you go there, you go at the pace of the water and that pace ties you into a flow that is older than life on this planet. Acceptance of that pace, even for a day, changes us, reminds us of other rhythms beyond the sound of our own heartbeats.

Jeff Rennicke, *River Days,* 1988

I like rivers,
Better than oceans,
For we see both sides.

Edwin Arlington Robinson, *Roman Bartholow,* 1923

The public must retain control of the great waterways. It is essential that any permit to obstruct them for reasons and on conditions that seem good at the moment should be subject to revision when changed conditions demand.

Theodore Roosevelt, 1908 Address

When a river—or the river of life—drops you to
your knees, don't ever enter a rapid tentatively.
And don't ever stop paddling.

Colleen Miniuk, *The Current Flows Exhibit*,
Santa Fe, New Mexico, 2001

Anything else you're interested in is not going to happen if
you can't breathe the air and drink the water.
Don't sit this one out. Do something.
You are by accident of fate alive at an absolutely critical
moment in the history of our planet.

Carl Sagan, *Pale Blue Dot*, 1994

Find some long river and follow it down.

Greg Brown, "Spring Wind" from *Dream Café*, 1992

### *Benedicto*

May your trails be crooked, winding, lonesome, dangerous, leading to the most amazing view. May your mountains rise into and above the clouds. May your rivers flow without end, meandering through pastoral valleys tinkling with bells, past temples and castles and poets towers into a dark primeval forest where tigers belch and monkeys howl, through miasmal and mysterious swamps and down into a desert of red rock, blue mesas, domes and pinnacles and grottos of endless stone, and down again into a deep vast ancient unknown chasm where bars of sunlight blaze on profiled cliffs, where deer walk across the white sand beaches, where storms come and go as lightning clangs upon the high crags, where something strange and more beautiful and more full of wonder than your deepest dreams waits for you—beyond that next turning of the canyon walls.

Edward Abbey, Preface to 1988 edition
of *Desert Solitaire.* 1968

Unless we change our approach to managing this precious and vital resource, the wars of the twenty-first century will be fought over water.

Dr. Ismail Serageldin,
Vice President of the World Bank, 1995.

A man may fish with the worm that hath eat of a king, and eat of the fish that hath fed of that worm.

William Shakespeare, *Hamlet,* 1623

To the lost man, to the pioneer penetrating a new country, to the naturalist who wishes to see the wild land at its wildest, the advice is always the same—follow a river. The river is the original forest highway. It is nature's own Wilderness Road.

Edwin Way Teale, *Journey Into Summer,* 1960

The finest workers in stone are not copper or steel tools, but the gentle touches of air and water working at their leisure with a liberal allowance of time.

Henry David Thoreau, *A Week on the Concord and Merrimack Rivers,* 1849

I chatter, chatter as I flow to join the brimming river
For men may come and men may go
But I go on forever

Lord Tennyson, *From the Brook,* 1855

I do not know much about gods; but I think that
the river is a strong brown god-sullen, untamed and
intractable, Patient to some degree, at first recognized
as a frontier; Useful, untrustworthy, as a conveyor
of commerce; Then only a problem confronting the
builder of bridges. The problem once solved,
the brown god is almost forgotten.

By the dwellers in cities-ever, however, implacable.
Keeping his seasons, and rages, destroyer,
reminder of what men choose to forget.

Unhonored, unpropitiated By worshippers of the
machine, but waiting, watching and waiting.

T. S. Eliot, *Four Quartets 3: The Dry Salvages,* 1943

It was kind of solemn, drifting down the big still river, laying on our backs looking up at the stars, and we didn't ever feel like talking loud, and it wasn't often that we laughed, only a little kind of low chuckle.

Mark Twain, *The Adventures of Huckleberry Finn,* 1885

. . . perhaps our grandsons, having never seen a wild river, will never miss the chance to set a canoe in singing waters . . . glad I shall never be young without wild country to be young in.

Aldo Leopold, *A Sand County Almanac,* 1949

Never turn your back on the ocean.

Captain Michael Feduccia, S/V Miss Cleo,
as told to the author

Under heaven nothing is more soft and yielding than water. Yet for attacking the solid and strong, nothing is better; it has no equal. The weak can overcome the strong; the supple can overcome the stiff. Under heaven everyone knows this, yet no one puts it into practice.

Lau Tzu, *Tao Te Ching,* 4th to 6th Century BC

If the Colorado River suddenly stopped flowing you would have two years of carryover capacity in the reservoirs before you had to evacuate most of Southern California and Arizona and a good portion of Colorado, New Mexico, Utah, and Wyoming.

Marc Reisner, *Cadillac Desert,* 1986

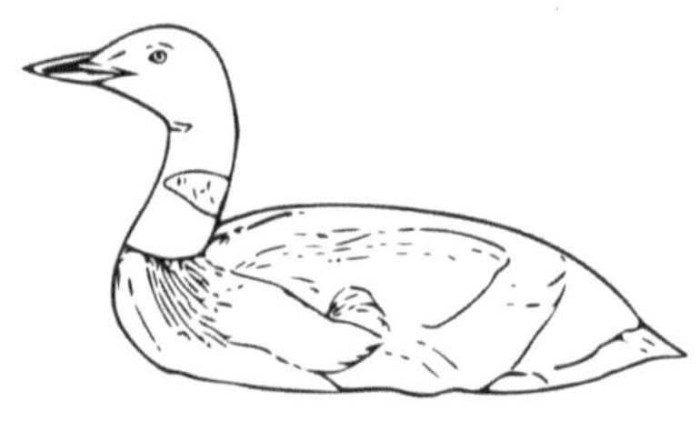

Chapter Seven

# Tribal Words *and* Proverbs

The waters tell of time. Always rivers run upon the earth and quench its thirst. Bright water carries our burdens across long distances. Without water we, and all that we know, would wither and die. We measure time by the flow of water as it passes us by. But in truth it is we who pass through time. Once I traveled on a great river though a canyon. The walls of the canyon were so old as to be timeless. There came a sunlit rain, and a double rainbow arched the river. There was mystery and meaning in my passage. I beheld things that others had beheld thousands of years ago. The earth is a place of wonder and beauty.

N. Scott. Momaday, *Earth Keeper: Reflections on the American Land,* 2020

In 1922, my tribe was subsistence living. The only way we could survive was through government rations on a piece of land that wasn't our traditional homeland. That's where we were at when the foundational Law of the River was created.

Daryl Vigil, Water and Tribes Initiative, Water administrator for the Jicarilla Apache Nation, on the impact of the Colorado River Compact of 1922 on Tribal water rights.

You can often find in rivers what you cannot find in oceans.

Native American Proverb

We call upon the waters that rim the earth,
horizon to horizon, that flow in our rivers and
streams, that fall upon our gardens and fields, and
we ask that they teach us and show us the way.

American Indian, Chinook Blessing Litany, *Earth Prayers from Around the World*, 1991

A bay is a noun only if water is dead. When
bay is a noun, it is defined by humans, trapped
between its shores and contained by the word.
But the verb wiikwegamaa—to be a bay—
releases the water from bondage and lets it live.
"To be a bay" holds the wonder that, for this
moment, the living water has decided to shelter
itself between these shores, conversing with
cedar roots and a flock of baby mergansers.

Robin Wall Kimmerer, *Braiding Sweetgrass*, 2013

Water is Life. It sustains people, plants, and animals. Scientists tell us that life began in water, and that both the earth's surface and the human body are about 70% water. When our bodies fade from this earth, our moisture once again becomes part of the great cycle of water... The sun warms the waters of the earth, the liquid evaporates into the atmosphere and becomes clouds. Clouds release life-giving moisture in the forms of rain, hail, sleet, and snow. Rain drops become aquifers, springs, streams and rivers which feed the lakes and oceans of the earth, and the process begins anew. Water connects all life together. It is sacred and essential to the well being of future generations. I pray that we recognize the stewardship responsibilities that we carry on this earth as human beings, and give thanks and honor the Wisdom demonstrated in the water cycle.

Ed Kabotie, Hopi musician, 2019

The Colorado River is the most endangered river in the
United States—also, it is a part of my body.

I carry a river. It is who I am: 'Aha Makav.
This is not metaphor.
When a Mojave says, Inyech 'Aha Makavch ithuum, we are
saying our name. We are telling a story of our existence.
The river runs through the middle of my body.

So far, I have said the word river in every stanza. I don't
want to waste water. I must preserve the river in my body.

Natalie Diaz, *The First Water is in the Body,* 2023

The frog does not drink up the pond in which he lives.

Native American Proverb

This River [The Klamath] is our Umbilical Cord. What feeds us and what nurtures us. This reciprocal relationship that we have with it, I would do anything for this river. Just like I would my own children. I would die for it. I would do anything before I give up on it.

Annelia Hillman, Klamath Justice Coalition, Yurok Tribal Member. Guardians of the River.

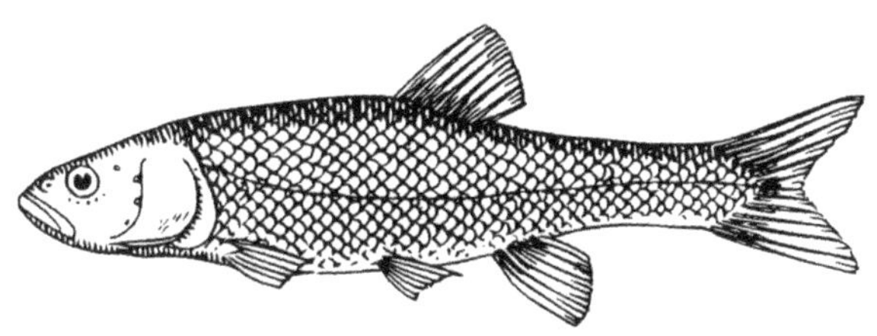

Every aspect of my life has been built around this river [The Klamath]. Whether it be teaching the next generation the skills of organizing, or whether it be providing food for my family.

Sammy Gensaw, Director, Yurok Ancestral Guard. Yurok Tribal Member. Guardians of the River.

Being that first Indigenous person on the Water Conservation Board, it really helped open my eyes on how other people make the decisions about water use within the state of Colorado... I have a greater understanding and respect for all of the water users in Colorado because they are very conscious about how water is being used and how water is being allocated... Tribal residents have to make the decisions if they can flush their toilets, if they have the water to wash their dishes, if they can take showers, on a daily basis. Other people in the basin don't have to make those decisions. They don't consciously think about paying for the water before they use it. Bridging those gaps, highlighting inequities that exist —it's all part of changing how the world views Tribes and Tribal water rights. Having Tribes in all of those conversations is really, really important. We are the senior water right holders. We are the first inhabitants of this continent. We are the first conservationists.

Lorelei Cloud, Vice Chairman of the Southern Ute Tribe, first indigenous person on the Colorado Water Conservation Board

We started noticing it [the drought] a while back, especially for our ceremony up on the mountain. Our springs are starting to dry up. The deer population has left. We have no deer now… Eventually, what's projected is the drought is going to get a little bit worse than what it is. We need to look at it now. Not 20 years down the road. Time is of the essence.

Manuel Heart, former Tribal Chairman,
Ute Mountain Ute Tribe

It's clear the shortage of water in the system is already impacting people who live at its fringes. The predictions for the future of this basin [the Colorado River] are extreme and as varied as the Salton Sea shoreline. As we move towards 2026 and the renegotiation of the Colorado River Compact, it's clear that human relationships are at the core of the solution. If we can't see eye to eye, there's going to be nothing left to look at.

Dr. Len Necefer, Diné, Navajo, *Outside TV*, 2025

How can I translate—not in words but in belief—that a river is a body, as alive as you or I, that there can be no life without it?

Natalie Diaz, *The First Water in in the Body*, 2023

They will try to hold on to the shore,
They will feel they're being torn
apart and will suffer greatly.
Know that the river has its destination.
The elders say we must let go of the shores,
Push off into the middle of the river,
Keep our eyes open and our heads above the water.
And I say, see who is there with you and celebrate.

Message from Hopi Elder, 2001

Nobody can be in good health if he does
not have fresh air, sunshine, and good water.

Chief Flying Hawk, *Firewater and Forked Tongues: A Sioux Chief Interprets U.S. History*, 1947

Mni Wiconi—Water is Life

Lakota Prophesy

When all the rivers are dried up, and the last tree cut down, only then will the white man realize that he can't eat money.

Cree Prophesy

There is a river flowing now very fast. It is so great and swift that there are those who will be afraid. They will try to hold on to the shore. They will feel they are torn apart and will suffer greatly.

Know the river has its destination. The elders say we must let go of the shore, push off into the middle of the river, keep our eyes open, and our heads above water. And I say, see who is in there with you and celebrate. At this time in history, we are to take nothing personally, Least of all ourselves. For the moment that we do, our spiritual growth and journey comes to a halt.

The time for the lone wolf is over. Gather yourselves! Banish the word struggle from you attitude and your vocabulary. All that we do now must be done in a sacred manner and in celebration.

We are the ones we've been waiting for.

Hopi Nation, Oraibi, Arizona

When I was a child, before falling asleep, my mother used to tell me stories. One of them was that beneath the city a river was sleeping—and that this river, running under all those streets, would one day rise in revolt and flood everything, bringing the city to an end. I was afraid.

Today I understand this ancestral prophecy, passed down from generation to generation so that we do not forget that the waters are made of sacred courage, patient strength, and a direction that cannot be negotiated. Secrets that we, Children of the Earth, formed from water and breathed into the winds, must claim in order to flow lovingly and with conviction.

The war is not lost: we continue to exist beneath the rubble of disenchanted societies. The waters, with their spirals of life, cleanse us and breathe their secrets into us. The rivers will awaken!

Suellen Ramos – Povo Indígena Goyá, Brazil, 2025

# PROVERBS

An ocean refuses no river.

South Asian Proverb

Filthy water cannot be washed.

West African Proverb

Don't throw away the old bucket until you
know whether the new one holds water.

Swedish Proverb

If you wish to drown, do not
torture yourself with shallow water.

Bulgarian Proverb

The deeper the waters are, the more still they run.

Korean Proverb

When the river is deepest it makes the least noise.

Proverb

You don't drown by falling into water.
You drown by staying there.

Proverb

When you drink the water, remember the spring.

Chinese Proverb

Enough shovels of earth – a mountain.
Enough pails of water – a river.

Chinese Proverb

Only dead fish go with the flow.

Proverb

Don't push a river, it flows by itself.

Chinese Proverb

Water is God's gift to living souls, to cleanse us,
to purify us, to sustain us and to renew us.

Hebrew Bridal Celebration Ceremony

All the water there will be, is…

Proverb

The mark of a successful man is one that has spent an entire day on the bank of a river without feeling guilty about it.

Chinese Proverb

To get clean water, one must go to the source.

French Proverb

A man of wisdom delights in water.

Confucius, *Analects*, 220 AD

*Gutta cavat lapidem.*
Dripping water hollows out a stone

Ovid, 8 AD

Before God created much else, His Spirit
moved upon the face of the waters.

*The Holy Bible, Genesis 1:2,* King James Version

Human nature is like water.
It takes the shape of its container.

Ancient Taoist Philosophy

On the last day of the feast, the great day, Jesus stood up and cried out, "If anyone thirsts, let him come to me and drink. Whoever believes in me as the Scripture as said, 'Out of his heart will flow rivers of living water.'"

*The Holy Bible, John 7:37-38,* King James Version

By means of water, we give life to everything.

*KORAN, 21:30*

What does a fish know of the water
it has swum in all its life?

Hebrew Proverb

The waters wear away the stones – אבנים שחקו מים

*Book of Job (Job 14:19), Hebrew Bible*

Human life is fleeting, like foam on water.

*Book of Job (Job 7:6), Hebrew Bible*

A dip in the holy river at Kumbh Mela
is a step closer to eternal peace.

YatraDham, on the Kumbh Mela,
the largest celebration of water on the planet

Different people call on [God] by different names: some as Allah, some as God, and others as Krishna, Siva, and Brahman. It is like the water in a lake. Some drink it at one place and call it 'jal', others at another place and call it 'pani', and still others at a third place and call it 'water'. The Hindus call it 'jal', the Christians 'water', and the Moslems 'pani'. But it is one and the same thing.

Ramakrishna, 1836-1886

In the sacred waters, our hearts unite, a journey of faith, through day and night with every dip, sins are washed away, In Kumbh Mela, we find our way.

YatraDham, on the Kumbh Mela,
the largest celebration of water on the planet

Water is the most perfect traveler because when it travels it becomes the path itself.

Turkish Proverb

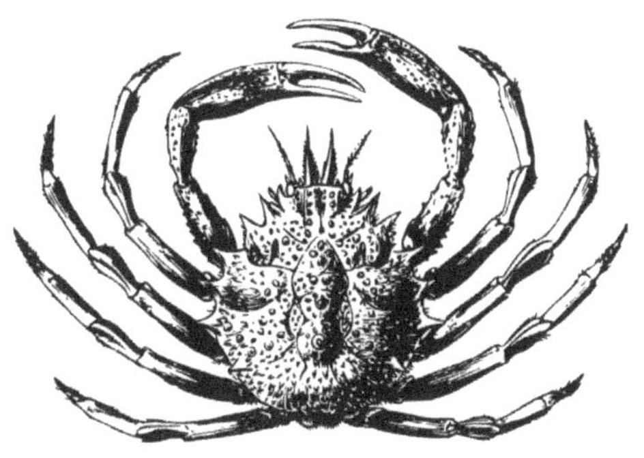

## SANSKRIT ON WATER

Water has a special place in Sanskrit, the most ancient language on Earth. The verses of Sanskrit show an abiding reverence and deep spiritual significance to water. Spoken and chronicled 5,000 years before the birth of Christ, they sing of the essential role of water in sustaining all forms of life and the cosmic order. Notable Sanskrit shlokas (verses) that mention water include:

Āpo hi sthā mayobhuvah

**The Rig Veda** praising the divine and life-giving properties of water.

Jalam eva jīvanam

Water is life itself. The fundamental importance of water for sustaining all life.

Toyam sarvasya prānah

Water is the essence of all living beings.

Apsu pratisthitāh

**The Upanishads**. The entire universe is established within the waters.

Chapter Eight

# Why Don’t Oysters Share Their Pearls?

May the countryside and the gliding valley streams content me. Lost to fame, let me love river and woodland.

Virgil, Georgics, Roman poet, circa 29 BC

If you gave me several million years, there would be nothing that did not grow in beauty if it were surrounded by water.

Jan Erik Vold, *What All The World Knows,* 1970

The progress of rivers to the ocean is not so rapid as that of man to error.

Voltaire, *A Philosophical Dictionary,* 1764

For those that don't think this pertains to them—if you eat winter vegetables in the U.S. or the West and use drinking faucets, or like electricity and power in Phoenix, LA, Vegas, Denver, and many more western cities and towns, the Colorado River runs through your life.

Peter McBride, *National Geographic* Photographer

The open space of democracy provides justice for all living things—plants, animals, rocks, and rivers, as well as human beings.

William Wordsworth, *The River Duddon: A Series of Sonnets,* 1820

The crisis of our diminishing water resources is just as severe (if less obviously immediate) as any wartime crisis we have ever faced. Our survival is just as much at stake as it was at the time of Pearl Harbor, or the Argonne, or Gettysburg, or Saratoga.

Jim Wright, *The Coming Water Famine*, 1966

No water, no life. No blue, no green.

Sylvia Earle, *Mission Blue*, 2014

Out there in the middle of the maelstrom the Eater awaits, heaving and gulping, its mouth like a giant clam's . . . its mind a frenzy of beige-colored rapid foam. A horrifying uproar, all things considered. Imagine floating through that nonsense in a life jacket.

Edward Abbey, *The Hidden Canyon – A River Journey,* 1999

Surrender to the flow of the River of Life, yet do not float down the river like a leaf or a log. While neither attempting to resist life nor to hurry it, become the rudder and use your energy to correct your course to avoid the whirlpools and undertow.

Jonathan Lockwood Huie,
*Daily Inspiration – Quotes for Joyful Living*, 2011

Among so many things, water has taught me that waves are just Mother Nature's way of restoring equilibrium.

Colleen Miniuk, photographer, artist, storyteller,
Southwest River Council, American Rivers

I understand that everything is connected, that all roads meet, and that all rivers flow into the same sea.

Paulo Coelho, *Aleph*, 2011

There are flood and drought
over the eyes and in the mouth,

dead water and dead sand
contending for the upper hand.

The parched eviscerate soil gapes at the vanity of toil,
laughs without mirth.
This is the death of the earth.

T. S. Eliot, *Four Quartets 4: Little Gidding*, 1943

Many a calm river begins as a turbulent waterfall,
yet none hurtles and foams all the way to the sea.

Mikhail Lermontov, *A Hero of Our Time*, 1840

Wondering if you are Love is like the
ocean wondering if it is water.

Sanober Kahn, *A Thousand Flamingos*, 2020

You can't stop the waves, but you can learn to surf.

Jon Kabat-Zan, *Full Catastrophe Living,* 1990

You can't cross the sea merely by
standing and staring at the water.

Rabindranath Tagore, *Stray Birds,* 1916

**Double Haiku**

Two Hydrogen
One Oxygen
Universal
Spring of yen and yang
The Sacred, sublime, you are
Sculptor of every lifetime

Jennifer Julian Blow, Artistic Director, Co-Founder of the Bywater Museum of Unnatural History in New Orleans

Heavy hearts, like heavy clouds in the sky,
are best relieved by the letting of a little water.

Christopher Morley, *The Romany Stain,* 1926

A drop of water, if it could write out its own history,
would explain the universe to us.

Lucy Larcom, *The Unseen Friend*, 1892

The wave does not need to die to become water.
She is already water.

Thich Nhat Hanh, *The Heart of the Buddha's Teaching: Transforming Suffering Into Peace, Joy, and Liberation*, 2015

When you do things from your soul,
you feel a river moving in you, a joy.

Rumi, 13th Century Persian poet, *The Essential Rumi*

I wish you water.

Wallace J. Nichols, *The Blue Mind: The Surprising Science That Shows How Being Near, In, On, or Under Water Can Make You Happier, Healthier, More Connected and Better at What You Do,* 2014

If you're not beside a real river, close your eyes, and sit down beside an imaginary one, a river where you feel comfortable and safe. Know that the water has wisdom, in its motion through the world, as much wisdom as any of us have. Picture yourself as the water. We are liquid; we innately share water's wisdom.

Eric Alan, Meditation Draws Its Power From the Water; *The Oregonian,* 2005

And I count myself more fortunate with each passing season to have recourse to these quiet, tree-strewn, untrimmed acres by the water. I would think it a sad commentary on the quality of American life if, with our pecuniary and natural abundance, we could not secure for our generation and those to come the existence of . . . a substantial remnant of a once great endowment of wild and scenic rivers.

William Anderson, Congressman from Tennessee, Arguing for passage of the Wild and Scenic Rivers Act, 1968

The marsh, to him who enters it in a receptive mood, holds, besides mosquitoes and stagnation, melody, the mystery of unknown waters, and the sweetness of Nature undisturbed by man.

Charles William Beebe, *Log of the Sun,* 1906

We labor long and earnestly for peace, because war threatens the survival of man. It is time we labored with equal passion to defend our environment. A polluted stream can be as lethal as a bullet.

Nevada Senator Alan Bible, *River of Life, Water: The Environmental Challenge*, 1970

Choosing to save a river is more often an act of passion than of careful calculation. You make the choice because the river has touched your life in an intimate and irreversible way, because you are unwilling to accept its loss.

David Bolling, *How to Save a River: Handbook for Citizen Action,* 1994

Any river is really the summation of the whole valley.

To think of it as nothing but water
is to ignore the greater part.

Hal Borland, *This Hill, This Valley,* 1957

It is difficult to find in life any event which so effectually condenses intense nervous sensation into the shortest possible space of time as does the work of shooting, or running an immense rapid. There is no toil, no heart breaking labour about it, but as much coolness, dexterity, and skill as man can throw into the work of hand, eye, and head; knowledge of when to strike and how to do it; knowledge of water and rock, and of the one hundred combinations which rock and water can assume—for these two things, rock and water, taken in the abstract, fail as completely to convey any idea of their fierce embracings in the throes of a rapid as the fire burning quietly in a drawing-room fireplace fails to convey the idea of a house wrapped and sheeted in Flames.

Sir William Francis Butler, *The Great Lone Land: The Northwest of America,* 1873

In a country where nature has been so lavish and where we have been so spendthrift of indigenous beauty, to set aside a few rivers in their natural state should be considered an obligation.

Senator Frank Church from Idaho, Arguing for passage of the Wild and Scenic Rivers Act, 1968

I know the sound the river makes,
by dawn, by night, by day

But can it stay me through tomorrows that
find me far away?

Ralph Conroy, Roger's River, *Field and Stream*, 1990

In spite of the durability of rock-walled canyons and the surging power of cataracting water, the wild river is a fragile thing—the most fragile portion of the wilderness country.

John Craighead, Biologist and one of the architects of the Wild and Scenic Rivers Act, 1965

We don't tend to ask where a lake comes from. It lies before us, contained and complete, tantalizing in its depth but not its origin. A river is a different kind of mystery, a mystery of distance and becoming, a mystery of source. Touch its fluent body and you touch far places. You touch a story that must end somewhere but cannot stop telling itself, a story that is always just beginning.

John Daniel, *Oregon Rivers*, 1997

I am beginning to understand that the stream the scientists are studying is not just a little creek. It's a river of energy that moves across regions in great geographic cycles. Here, life and death are only different points on a continuum. The stream flows in a circle through time and space, turning death into life across coastal ecosystems, as it has for more than a million years. But such streams no longer flow in the places where most of us live.

Kathleen Dean Moore and Jonathan W. Moore, "The Gift of Salmon," *Discover* Magazine, 2003

The ocean begins where the raindrop falls. To care for the sea, we must honor the sky, the rivers, and the mountains.

Vicki Nichols Goldstein, Founder, Inland Ocean Coalition

I stand by the river and I know that it has been here yesterday and will be here tomorrow and that therefore, since I am part of its pattern today, I also belong to all its yesterdays and will be a part of all its tomorrows. This is a kind of earthly immortality, a kinship with rivers and hills and rocks, with all things and all creatures that have ever lived or ever will live or have their being on the earth. It is my assurance of an orderly continuity in the great design of the universe.

Virginia Eifert, *River World: Wildlife of the Mississippi*, 1959

For an instant, as I bobbed into the channel, I had the sensation of sliding down the vast, tilted face of the continent. It was then that I felt the cold needles of Alpine springs at my fingertips and the warmth of the Gulf pulling me southward. Moving with me, leaving its taste upon my mouth and spouting under me in dancing springs of sand, was the immense body of the continent itself, flowing like the river was flowing, grain by grain, mountain by mountain, down to the sea. I was streaming over ancient sea beds thrust aloft where giant reptiles had once sported; I was wearing down the face of time.

Loren Eiseley, "Four Quartets,"
in *The Immense Journey*, 1953

The woods are made for the hunters of dreams,
The brooks for the fishers of song;
To the hunters who hunt for the gunless game
The streams and the woods belong.

Sam Walter Foss, *The Bloodless Sportsman,* 1898

What would the world be,
once bereft of wet and wilderness?

Let them be left,
O let them be left, wilderness and wet;
Long live the weeds and the wilderness yet.

Gerard Manley Hopkins, *Inversnaid,* 1881

Rivers have what man most respects and longs for in his own life—a capacity for renewal and replenishment, continual energy, creativity, cleansing.

John Kauffman, *A Look At Our North Atlantic Rivers,* 1973

(A Montana statute) holds that a river has a right to overwhelm its banks and inundate its floodplain. Well, that's interesting, because it's not a right that we assign to the river. The river has earned it through centuries of deluging and shaping the floodplain, and the floodplain has a right to its rampaging river. They've earned their rights through a kind of reciprocal action.

Dan Kemmis, *Harper's* Magazine, 1991

Water is fluid, soft, and yielding. But water will wear away rock, which is rigid and cannot yield. As a rule, whatever is fluid, soft, and yielding will overcome whatever is rigid and hard. This is another paradox: What is soft is strong.

Lao Tzu, *Tao Te Ching,* 4th to 6th Century BC

When time comes for us to again rejoin the infinite stream of water flowing to and from the great timeless ocean, our little droplet of soulful water will once again flow with the endless stream.

William Marks, *The Holy Order of Water,* 2001

Beside the grand history of the glaciers and their own, the mountain streams sing the history of every avalanche or earthquake and of snow, all easily recognized by the human ear, and every word evoked by the falling leaf and drinking deer, beside a thousand other facts so small and spoken by the stream in so low a voice the human ear cannot hear them.

John Muir, *Mountain Thoughts,* 1938

In every glass of water we drink, some of the water has already passed through fishes, trees, bacteria, worms in the soil, and many other organisms, including people... Living systems cleanse water and make it fit, among other things, for human consumption.

Elliott Norse, *Animal Extinctions,* 1993

Our precious heritage of natural and unspoiled beauty and unpolluted streams, once exhausted and destroyed, can never be replaced. . . . We have a golden opportunity to save the few remaining scenic and wild rivers as part of our nation's heritage for this and coming generations.

Alvin O'Konski, Congressman from Wisconsin about the St. Croix River, 1968

When we save a river, we save a major part of an ecosystem, and we save ourselves as well because of our dependence—physical, economic, spiritual—on the water and its community of life.

Tim Palmer, *The Wild and Scenic Rivers of America,* 1993

I hadn't had a bite to eat since yesterday, so Jim he got out some corn-dodgers and buttermilk, and pork and cabbage and greens—there ain't nothing in the world so good when it's cooked right—and whilst I eat my supper we talked and had a good time. . . .We said there warn't no home like a raft, after all. Other places do seem so cramped up and smothery, but a raft don't. You feel mighty free and easy and comfortable on a raft

Mark Twain, *The Adventures of Huckleberry Finn,* 1885

The way of a canoe is the way of the wilderness, and of a freedom almost forgotten.

Sigurd F. Olson, *The Singing Wilderness,* 1956

Wonderful how completely everything in wild nature fits into us, as if truly part and parent of us. The sun shines not on us but in us. The rivers flow not past, but through us, thrilling, tingling, vibrating every fiber and cell of the substance of our bodies, making them glide and sing. The trees wave and the flowers bloom in our bodies as well as our souls, and every bird song, wind song, and; tremendous storm song of the rocks in the heart of the mountains is our song, our very own, and sings our love.

John Muir, *Mountain Thoughts,* 1938

Originality is unexplored territory. You get there by carrying a canoe – you can't take a taxi. You have to leave the city of your comfort and go into the wilderness of your intuition. You cannot get there by bus, only by hard work, risking and by not quite knowing what you are doing.

Alan Alda, Actor, Commencement address at Connecticut College, 1980

Don't push the river—it flows by itself.

Fritz Perls, *Gestalt Therapy Verbatim,* 1969

No one will believe it, but this river (the Platte) is more exciting than football.

James Michener, *Centennial*, 1974

## *The Humor of Water*

What do you get when you throw
a billion books into the ocean?

A title wave.

What did the ocean say to the beach?

Nothing, it just waved.

What did the fish say when it hit the wall?

Damn!

Where can you find an ocean with no water?

On a map!

Why did the ocean break up with the pond?

She thought he was too shallow.

Why are oceans so meticulous?

They like to be pacific.

What runs, but never walks?
What has a mouth, but never speaks?
A River!

Why don't oysters share their pearls?

Because they are shellfish.

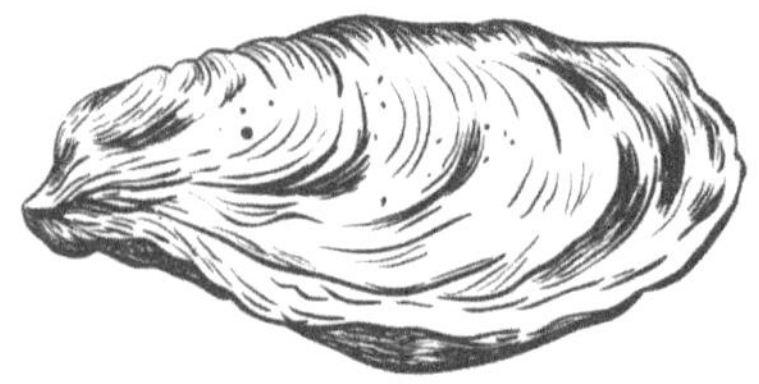

# Boatman's Prayer

## Raging River Lonely Trail

by Vaughn Short

Dear Lord here on this river bank
Before we launch today
Please listen for a moment
To what a boatman has to say

Now I don't claim to be a saint
And my souls not lily white
Sometimes I yield to temptation
Sometimes I drink too much at night

Down here I'm not an angel
Don't even want to talk about the town
With all its woes and pitfalls
And the things that get you down

So I'm really in no position
To ask for much from you
But if you could see the way
Please try and hear me through

Life down here's a pleasure
And there's beauty everywhere
So I'm really not complaining
In my humble little prayer

The thing I'm trying to get across
In my stublin' bumblin' way
Is a boatman he's not really bad
No matter what they say

But a boatman's life's not easy
Although I'm not trying to alibi
There's no turning back up river
There's no use to even try

Whatever lies before you
You've got to see it through
You can't stop half way
And back off and start anew

Its just things aren't as easy
As they look to those outside
It's more than jumping in a boat
And going for a ride

Now I'm not too worried
About what's down the way
'Cause I've done this many times before
When I didn't even pray

Oh! I don't take it lightly!
I've always got to know
There's an old lion a roarin'
In the river down below

But we'll make it through the rapids
There'll be no problem there
That's really not the reason
For me to say this prayer

The reason I'm a talkin'
and it's not easy for me to say
Just please don't view us boatmen
In the ordinary way

I love this world you made us
And I love the rivers too
I like the things that are simple
And I like the work I do

But could you sort of look the other way
And a few small things forgive?
For it's a little different
This kind of life I live

I have no neighbors watching
To see what I do each day
So it's just a little easier
To stray off the narrow way

Now I have no church to go to
They just aren't built down here
But I see your walls and canyons
And I feel you very near

Now I'm standing here a rattlin'
I've talked for quite a spell
I still can't seem to get across
What I'm try to tell

It's just please try to overlook
Some of the things I do
I may not be like your other children
But I feel very close to you

Amen

Chapter Nine

# Quotes That Were Not

After fact checking all of the quotes in this book, several were found to be dubious and incorrect attributions or downright hoaxes.

*Whiskey is for drinking. Water is for fighting.*

Attributed to Mark Twain.

While it sounds like something he might say, there is no actual record of it. A very common quote liberally used in the water profession among engineers, policy makers, farmers, environmentalists and the like. The Twain Estate has no source in his writings or correspondence of this quote. Brought to my attention by historian Patty Limerick.

*No man ever steps in the same river twice, for it's not the same river, and he's not the same man.*

Attributed to Hercalitus

There is no record of him saying or writing this, though it hasn't prevented it from proliferating throughout many texts that use it as a quotation. While Heraclitus is famous for this statement, his original writings do not exist, and his words only survive in fragments quoted by later ancient authors. The versions that have been passed down include:

In his dialogue Cratylus, Plato quotes Heraclitus as saying, "you could not step into the same river twice"

Plutarch's version states, "It is impossible to step twice in the same river".

The Roman philosopher Seneca presented a more detailed interpretation of the sentiment, which aligns more closely with the longer form of the quote today. The full phrasing "...for it's not the same river, and he's not the same man" is a synthesis that has been refined and popularized over centuries.

*If a man fails to honor the rivers,*
*he shall not gain the life from them.*

Attributed to The Code of Hammurabi, 1780 BC

This quote is a modern interpretation that has been incorrectly attributed to the Code of Hammurabi. The wording is not authentic. The Code of Hammurabi's language is legalistic, not poetic or spiritual in the way this quote suggests. The actual laws were very different. While the Code of Hammurabi did involve rivers, it was in the context of specific laws, such as a "trial by ordeal" for serious accusation. For instance, the accused had to jump in the river. If he died, he was guilty. If he lived he was innocent.

*Boundaries don't protect rivers, people do.*

Attributed to Aristotle

While this quote is widely attributed to Aristotle, there is no source or record of him writing or saying it. While poetic, and true, it is likely a modern invention.

*Water is the soul of the Earth.*

Attributed to W.H. Auden.

No source found and doesn't appear in writings. W.H Auden Society, "A Few Things Auden Never Wrote (or Did)"

*The River is afraid when entering the ocean.*

*They say that before entering the sea, the river trembles with fear; He looks back at the entire journey, the peaks and mountains, the long and winding road that crossed between jungles and towns, and sees in front of him an ocean so large that entering it can only mean disappearing forever. But there is no other way. The river cannot return. Nobody can come back. Going back is impossible in existence. There is no other way, the river cannot return. The river needs to accept its nature and enter the ocean. Only by entering the ocean will the fear dissipate. Because only then will the river know that it is not about disappearing into the ocean, but about becoming an ocean.*

Attributed to Khalil Gibran, A Metaphor about Life.

While widely attributed to Gibran, there is no source of him saying it. There is, however, a similar text written in Beyond Enlightenment by Osho. Osho was a religious cult leader and bioterrorist who lived in Oregon. There's a Netflix Documentary about him called *Wild Wild Country*.

*It is very easy for me to calculate the positions of the sun, moon, and any planet, but I cannot calculate the positions of water particles as they move through the earth.*

Attributed to Galileo

The quote is not a known saying by Galileo Galilei. It appears to be a misattribution or a modern paraphrase of a similar, more famous quote by Isaac Newton. The actual quote by Isaac Newton is: "I can calculate the motion of heavenly bodies, but not the madness of people." This quote is reportedly from Newton after he lost a significant amount of money investing in the South Sea Company stock bubble in 1720.

*When I sit here by the sea and listen to the sound of waves, I feel free from all obligations and people of this world.*

Attributed to Henry Thoreau

While widely attributed to Thoreau, this quote does not appear in any of his published works. This is likely a more modern quote falsely attributed to Thoreau.

## Chapter Ten

# Reflections From Water

by Matthew Moseley

After a lifetime of open-water adventure swimming, not only have I spent countless hours in the water, I've had a lot of time to think about it. Across bodies of water around the world, each molecule may be the same H2O, but every body is different. The water has shared with me a number of universal lessons:

> Find people who are your *thalweg*—those who keep you in the deepest, strongest current.
>
> Fear, not fatigue, may be the open water swimmer's greatest enemy.
>
> Even with all the planning, training and putting together a great team, I've come to realize that sometimes in open water swimming, as in life, you end up on the wrong island. Expect the Unexpected.

Water demands a tricky balance: Too little, and you die. Too much, and you die.

Transformation happens out there in the canyons. On the water. On any adventure really. Take experience, hardship, elation, top it off with a dollop of love and friendship and, behold! *Meaning*.

Whether it's a regular team workout or an epic open water swim, the swimmer must prepare to be changed. Swimming, like good listening, or good living, requires being ready for all you may encounter and being open to change.

Dehydration in water is an awful irony.

The techniques of conditioning your mind apply just as much to everyday life as to endurance swimming: Setting a big goal and training for it. Doing the hard work. Preparing and perseverance.

## The River Doesn't Argue

The river doesn't debate its course. It simply follows it. When I'm swimming in the current, I'm reminded that progress isn't always about force—it's about flow. Water teaches us the art of persistence with grace. It finds a way through, under, around—never in defiance, but always in motion. In a world obsessed with control, the river reminds us: the most powerful way to lead is often to yield.

When I slip into a lake at dawn, the world stills. My arms begin to stroke, my breath slows, and I become part of something older than language. Water doesn't ask who you are or what you've done. It asks only that you be present. That's the invitation of water—not to conquer, but to merge with the moment.

**Qualities of Water to Apply to Life:**

**Adaptable.** Water takes the shape of whatever holds it—never losing its essence.

**Persistent.** Over time, it smooths stone and carves canyons.

**Reflective.** When still, water reveals the truth of our inner lives.

**Life-giving.** Without water, nothing thrives. Let your presence nourish others.

**In motion.** Stagnant water breeds decay. Flow brings renewal.

**Humble.** Water seeks the lowest point, and in doing so, becomes the source of all life.

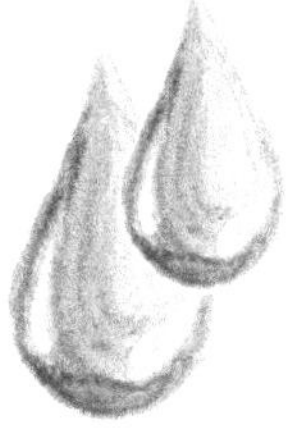

# Afterword

# What We Can do to Protect Water

By Michael Fiebig

"Anything else you're interested in is not going to
happen if you can't breathe the air and drink the water.
Don't sit this one out. Do something.
You are by accident of fate alive at an absolutely
critical moment in the history of our planet."

Carl Sagan, *Pale Blue Dot,* 1994

Through the collective wisdom contained in these pages, ***Words on Water*** reminds us of the ubiquitousness of water in our lives. There is of course no other element more important to life on Earth. Additionally, water permeates our arts and culture, our food, our recreational activities, and our mental health, where we live, and what we consider beautiful in this world. It is critical to both our economy and our ways of life, and when water is degraded or access to it is blocked, it can be a driver of inequity. Likewise, water—in the form of floods and droughts—continues to be one of the ways in which our changing climate is felt most acutely.

It's said that when you work on water, you work on everything. I can imagine a future where water no longer needs protection or defense, only stewardship, but to get there we need to connect more people to water and to one another. Water stewards need your help to make this future a reality.

Thousands of organizations around the world work to preserve and protect clean drinking water, and the water in our rivers, lakes, oceans, and aquifers. These organizations need your help and support. Likewise, armed with the quotes and inspiration contained in the book, we now have another tool to help us more fully integrate water stewardship into our daily lives and the lives of those around us. Use them to start conversations. To signify important moments. To inspire awe and action. And to connect. Because when we are connected to our water we can't help but want to protect it.

*Michael Fiebig is the Director of River Protection for the Southwest U.S. at American Rivers. No stranger to marathon adventures, Mike and his wife, Jenny, completed a 5-month, 1800-mile source-to-sea journey on the Green and Colorado rivers in a purpose-built dory in 2018. They live in Durango, Colorado.*

# Water Conservation Resources

**To learn more, check out the following organizations:**

**Your Local Watershed Group** – Find your local watershed group and get in touch. Your local river, lake, wetland, or estuary surely has one, and a little digging online should get you there. If it doesn't, maybe you should start one?

**American Rivers** – I might be biased, but there is no other organization in the U.S. working for a future when every river is clean and healthy for people and wildlife, across the country. Because life depends on rivers. And we need your help to make that future a reality. See: americanrivers.org

**Surfrider Foundation** – The Surfrider Foundation is dedicated to the protection and enjoyment of the world's ocean, waves, and beaches, for all people, through a powerful activist network. See: surfrider.org

**American Whitewater** – American Whitewater advocates for the preservation and protection of whitewater rivers throughout the United States and connects the interests of human-powered recreational river users with ecological and science-based data to achieve its goals. See: americanwhitewater.org

**Trout Unlimited** – Trout Unlimited brings together diverse interests to care for and recover rivers and streams so our children can experience the joy of wild and native trout and salmon. See: tu.org

**Universal Access to Clean Water for Tribal Communities (UACW)** – UACW focuses on closing the water gap in Indian Country and holding the federal government accountable under its treaty and trust responsibilities to Tribes. To lay this groundwork, UACW investigates the legal, economic, and historic impediments to water access for Tribal communities and documents solution pathways to address the lack of access to clean drinking water for Tribal communities. See: tribalcleanwater.org

**Dig Deep** – Dig Deep's community-led projects bring clean, hot and cold running water into American homes. They also invest in research, advocacy, and workforce development to close the Water Gap once and for all. See: digdeep.org

**Water for People** – Water for People envisions a world where every person has access to reliable and safe water and sanitation services. It promotes the development of high-quality drinking water and sanitation services, accessible to all, and sustained by strong communities, businesses, and governments. See: waterforpeople.org

**International Rivers** – International Rivers protects rivers around the world and defends the rights of communities that depend on them. See: internationalrivers.org

**Inland Ocean Coalition** – We often think that to protect the ocean, you have to be near the ocean. But we all have a direct impact on the cycles of life in the ocean—no matter where we live. The changes we need to make to address the largest threats facing our seas—lowering carbon emissions, reducing plastic and other pollution, protecting our fisheries, safeguarding watersheds, promoting marine protected areas, and fighting for legislation that supports our ocean, waterways, and climate—can happen from anywhere in the world.

The Inland Ocean Coalition is working to build ocean conservation constituencies around the US. We hope you'll join us to protect the ocean we all love.

**5 Gyres Institute** – Leveraging the power of science, advocacy, and community to drive innovative solutions to plastic pollution.

Plastic can be found in every corner of the globe. Plastics contaminate the environment, entangle countless marine and land animals, and are inextricably linked to the climate crisis, as plastics production is driving massive increases in fossil fuel infrastructure. With direct links between the plastic crisis and the climate crisis, addressing plastic pollution globally must be a major environmental priority. 5 Gyres continues to lead with scientific research to drive upstream solutions through education, advocacy, and community building.

# Acknowledgements

First off I should offer a word of gratitude to all of the authors and sources who have cared to write about water throughout the history of literature. A hearty thank you to Fletcher Lucas, a student at University of Colorado and avid adventurer, for diligently fact checking all of the sources and quotes. My sister, Mary Lobdell, who has worked on every one of my books, was an early supporter and reader of the project. I am grateful for the work of American Rivers, where I serve on the Presidents National Council, and NOLS–The National Outdoor Leadership School–who were a generous source of material from the archives and newsletters.

Others who provided quotes were Mike Fiebig, Mike Dehoff, Matt Rice, Fred Phillips, Vick Nichols Goldstein, Matthew McKinney, Colleen Miniuk, Kate Ryan, Sam Carter, Ramsey Kropf, Zane Kessler, Daryl Vigil, Gad Reich, Michael Feduccia, and Liza Getches.

A particular heartfelt note of gratitude to Liza Getches and Peter Olivo for their support and love throughout many years. I worked on the book at her family's cabin off Magnolia Road above Boulder called Las Abuelas. I edited in the Writing Tower of Liza's father, legendary Tribal water rights attorney and scholar, David Getches. As I looked out onto the Continental Divide, I should like to think I was channeling him as I read the quotes.

I am eternally grateful to my publisher CG Sports Publishing and Mike Nicloy for his enthusiastic support.

Lastly, my family is my river. A special thank you to Charlie, Amelia, and Kristin, our water. We are very blessed.

*Photo credit to Peter McBride*

# About the Author

Matthew L. Moseley is a communication strategist, author, speaker, and world-record adventure swimmer. He has spent his career at the intersection of public policy, business, and government and has managed many public affairs projects and campaigns for organizations and companies.

He works with organizations such as the Upper Colorado River Commission, the Water and Tribes Initiative, American Rivers, the Colorado Water Trust, the Colorado River District, the Getches Wilkinson Center and others. He is the author of four books.

He has completed five first-ever record adventure swims and is the subject of the documentary, ***Dancing in the Water*** about his 25-mile swim across Lake Pontchartrain in New Orleans. The short film ***Silent River*** documented his 40-mile swim down the Green River in the Colorado River Basin.

He serves on the President's Council for American Rivers and is member of the Advisory Board of the Center for Leadership at the University of Colorado at Boulder. He lives in Boulder, Colorado.

www.MatthewLMoseley.net

# Appendix of Sources for Quotations

Abbey, Edward. *Desert Solitaire: A Season in the Wilderness.* University of Arizona Press, 1968, 1988.

Abbey, Edward. "Joy, Shipmates, Joy!" High Country News, September 1976.

Abbey, Edward & Blaustein, John. *The Hidden Canyon - A River Journey.* Chronicle Books, April 1, 1999. Pg. 64, 115.

Alan, Eric. "Meditation Draws Its Power From the Water." From *The Oregonian.* September 11, 2005.

Alda, Alan. Actor. Commencement address at Connecticut College, 1980.

Ambrose, Stephen. *Undaunted Courage.* Simon & Schuster, 1996.

American Rivers, et. al. *Rivers at Risk: Concerned Citizen's Guide To Hydropower.* Island Press, 2013.

Anderson, William. Tennessee congressman. Arguing for the passage of the Wild and Scenic Rivers Act, 1968.

Angelou, Maya. "On the Pulse of Morning." Speech, Inauguration of Bill Clinton, 1993.

Ashworth, William. *Nor Any Drop to Drink.* Summit Books, 1982.

Asimov, Isaac. *Isaac Asimov's Book of Science and Nature Quotations.* Grove Pr, 1990.

Atwood, Margaret. *The Penelopiad.* Knopf Canada, 2005.

Auden, W. H. "First Things First." *The New Yorker*, March 9, 1957.

Aurelius, Marcus & Xylander, Wilhelm (Editio Princeps). *Meditations.* Walter Scott, 1887. 180 CE.

Austen, Jane. *Emma.* John Murray, 1816.

Ball, Philip. *Life's Matrix: A Biography of Water.* University of California Press, 2000.

Bangs, Richard. *Rivergods, Exploring the World's Great Wild River.* Sierra Club Books, 1986.

Beebe, Charles William. *Log of the Sun: A Chronicle of Nature's Year.* Garden City Publishing, 1906.

Bennett, Jeffrey, Ph.D in Astrophysics from the University of Colorado Boulder. Author and swimmer.

Berry, Wendell. *The Unforeseen Wilderness.* Counterpoint Press, 1972.

Beuchner, Frederick. *The Sacred Journey.* Pg. 25. HarperOne, October 11, 1991.

Beyoncé. Burke, Ed. Year of 4. Vevo, 2011.

Bible, Alan. Senator of Nevada, 1954-1974.

Blake, Peter & Sefton, Alan. *The Last Great Adventure Of Peter Blake: With the Seamaster and Blake Expeditions from Antarctica to the Amazon : Sir Peter Blake's Logbooks.* Sheridan House, 2004.

Blow, Jennifer Julian, Artistic Director, Bywater Museum of Unnatural History, New Orleans, Louisiana. Original composition for *Words on Water.*

Bolling, David. *How to Save a River: A Handbook For Citizen Action.* Island Press, 1994.

Borland, Hal. *This Hill, This Valley.* Johns Hopkins University Press, 1957.

Bowie, David & Crowe, Cameron. "Ground Control to Davy Jones." *Rolling Stone Magazine* Issue 206. February 12, 1976.

Boyle, Hal. Pulitzer Prize-winning columnist for the Associated Press from the 1930s until his death in 1974.

Brashares, Ann. "The ocean was the best place, of course." Facebook, October 5, 2012.

Brower, David. *Let the Mountains Talk, Let the Rivers Run: A Call to Those Who Would Save the Earth.* Harper Collins, 1995.

Brown, Greg. "Spring Wind," from *Dream Cafe*, Red House, 1992.

Brown, Rob. Wheeler School, Providence R.I., *Science Findings* Magazine, 2004

Buechner, Frederick. *The Sacred Journey: A Memoir of Early Days – A Spiritual Chronicle of How God Speaks in Everyday Moments from Childhood to Seminary.* HarperOne, 1991.

Buckley, Will & Riley, Diego. *What the River Knows*, Glen Canyon Institute 2025. Includes Lee, Katie; Necefer, Dr. Len; Klemme, Cheyenne; & Dominy, Floyd.

Buffalo Joe. Source Unknown.

Burke, James Lee. *Creole Belle*. Pg. 3. Simon & Schuster, 2012.

Butler, Sir William Francis. *The Great Lone Land: the North-West of America.* Oxford University Press, 1873.

Cain, Stanley. Speech "The Estuary a 'Happy' Land." 1963 Bays and Estuaries Conference.

Caitlin, George. *Letters and Notes on the North American Indians.* JG Press, 1841.

Carney, Julia. "Little Things," 1881.

Cheever, John. "The Swimmer." Originally published in *The New Yorker*, July 10, 1964.

Childs, Craig. *The Desert Cries: A Season of Flash Floods in a Dry Land.* Arizona Highways, 2002.

Childs, Craig. *The Secret Knowledge of Water.* Back Bay Books, Mar 1, 2000. Pg. XIII.

Chōmei, Kamo no & Keene Donald (Translator). *Hōjōki.* 1212. Penguin Classics, 1967.

Church, Frank. Senator from Idaho, arguing for the passage of the Wild and Scenic Rivers Act (1968). Debate on S. 119, The Wild and Scenic Rivers Bill, October 2, 1967.

Cloud, Lorelei, found in Romero, Jared. "When We Pray, We Always Pray About Water." Walton Family Foundation, 2024.

Coelho, Paulo. *Aleph.* HarperCollins, 2011. Pg. 156.

Coleridge, Samuel Taylor. *The Rime of the Ancient Mariner.* J. & A. Arch, 1798.

Confucius, Analects, 220 AD

Conrad, Joseph. *The Mirror of the Sea.* Wildside Pr, 1906.

Conrad, Joseph. "The Secret Sharer." Harper's Magazine, August and September 1910.

Conroy, Ralph. "Roger's River." From *Field and Stream* Magazine, August 1990 Issue.

Cousteau, Jacques-Yves and Schiefelbein, Susan. *The Human, The Orchid, and The Octopus.* Bloomsbury USA, October 30, 2007.

Cox, Lynne. Quoted by her, in the book: *Swimming to Antarctica: Tales of a Long-Distance Swimmer,* Mariner Books, 2005.

Craighead, John. "The River Called." From *Naturalist* Magazine, Autumn 1965 issue.

Craighead, John. Biologist and founder of the Craighead Environmental Research Institute along with his brother. This Institute paved the way for the passing of the National Wild and Scenic Rivers bill of 1965 as well as the Wild and Scenic Rivers Act.

Crawford, Stanley. *Mayordomo: Chronicle of an Acequia in Northern New Mexico.* UNM Press, 1988.

Cullney, John. *Wilderness Conservation Magazine.* September-October 1990.

Cummings, E.E. From Poem "maggie and milly and molly and may". 1958

Cunningham, Ron. "Lake Okeechobee: a Disaster Waiting to Happen." *Ocala Star Banner.* September 2023.

Curtis, G. W. *Lotus Eating: Hudson and Rhine.* Harper, 1877.

Cuthbert Soup. Swallow, Gerry. *Another Whole Nother Story.* Bloomsbury USA. Childrens, 2010. Epigraph. Cuthbert Soup is the Pen name for Gerry Swallow, author of the Whole Nother Story children's books series

Daniel, John. *Oregon Rivers.* Westcliffe Pub, 1997.

Davis, Wade. *Magdalena, River of Dreams.* Knopf, 2020.

Da Vinci, Leonardo. In the original Italian, "L'acqua è la forza motrice di tutta la natura." No source found for this quote, though it is likely from one of his journals, perhaps his study of water.

Da Vinci, Leonardo. *Notebooks.* Reynal & Hitchcock, 1939.

De Mello, Anthony. *One Minute Wisdom.* PRH Christian Publishing, 1988. Pg. 89.

DeHoff, Mike. "An interview with Mike DeHoff of the Returning Rapids Project." Northern Arizona University, 2022.

De Saint-Exupery, Antoine. *Wind, Sand, and Stars.* Reynal and Hitchcock, 1939.

De Villiers, Marc. *Water: The Fate of Our Most Precious Resource.* Harper One, 2001.

Diaz, Natalie. "The First Water is in the Body." *Emergence Magazine.* 2023.

Dickey, James. *Deliverance.* Houghton Mifflin, 1970.

Digby, Edward. *The Art of Swimming* Public Domain, 1587. First book ever published on swimming. In *Ocean* (2020), Steve Mentz calls Digby's work the "central historical text marking the upsurge of interest in swimming in early modern England." Then Lord Byron, Benjamin Franklin and others followed. Woodcuts courtesy of the Wellcome Collection. Collected from https://publicdomainreview.org/collection/the-art-of-swimming-1587/

Dinesen, Isak. "The Deluge at Norderney." *Seven Gothic Tales.* Harrison Smith & Robert Hass, 1934.

Doerr, Anthony. *Cloud Cuckoo Land.* Fourth Estate, September 28, 2021.

Dyer, John. Welsh Poet. "Grongar Hill." 1726.

Earle, Dr. Sylvia. Marine biologist and oceanographer. *The World is Blue: How Our Fate and the Oceans are One.* National Geographic, 2009.

Earle, Sylvia. *Mission Blue* (documentary). Netflix, 2014.

Ehrlich, Gretel. *Islands, The Universe, Home.* Penguin Publishing, 1991.

Eifert, Virginia. *River World: Wildlife of the Mississippi.* Dodd, Mead, & Company, 1959.

Eiseley, Loren C. "The Flow of the River." *The American Scholar*, vol. 22, no. 4, pp. 451–58. JSTOR, 1953.

Eliot, T. S. *Four Quartets.* Harcourt, 1943.

Eliot, T. S. Introduction to:
Twain, Mark. *The Adventures of Huckleberry Finn.* Chanticleer Press Edition, 1950.

Emerson, Ralph Waldo. *Nature.* James Munroe and Company in 1836.

Erickson, Victoria. *Edge of Wonder.* Enrealment Press, 2015

Estes, Clarissa Pinkola Ph.D. *Women Who Run With the Wolves: Myths and Stories of the Wild Woman Archetype.* Chapter 10, pg 323.

Farinango, Maria Virginia & Resau, Laura. *The Queen of Water.* Ember, 2012.

Fedarko, Kevin. *The Emerald Mile: The Epic Story of the Fastest Ride in History Through the Heart of the Grand Canyon.* Scribner, May 7, 2013. Pg. 319, 354.

Fedarko, Kevin. *A Walk in the Park: The True Story of a Spectacular Misadventure in the Grand Canyon.* Scribner, May 28, 2024. Pg. 345.

Feduccia, Michael. Told to Matt Moseley on Feduccia's boat, May 4, 2024.

Fiebig, Mike. Director, Southwest River Protection Program, American Rivers.

Fiebig, Mike. Randall, Cassidy. "Humans Killed Cataract Canyon. It Brought Itself Back to Life. Damming the Colorado River wiped out a magnificent stretch of rapids for half a century. Now, incredibly, they're returning — on their own." *Rolling Stone Magazine*, February 18, 2024.

Foss, Sam Walter. "The Bloodless Sportsman." From the *Journal of Education.* Vol. XLVIII, July 14, 1898.

Franklin, Benjamin. *Memoirs of Benjamin Franklin.* J. Parson's, 1791.

Franklin, Benjamin. *Poor Richard's Almanack.* The U.S.C. Publishing Company, 1914. Stanza 627.

Freeman, James Dillet. "Rivers Hardly Ever." From *The Story of Unity.* Unity, 1954.

Gargan, Edward. *The River's Tale: A Year on the Mekong.* Knopf Doubleday Publishing Group, January 22, 2002. Pg. 8.

Gerber, Linda. *Death by Bikini.* Puffin Books, 2008.

Getches, David. *Water Law in a Nutshell.* Pg. 20. West Academic Publishing, November 13, 2008.

Gandhi, Mahatma. mkgandhi.org. https://www.mkgandhi.org/articles/environment1.php

Gibran, Kahlil. "Oneness." *The Essential Khalil Gibran.* Pg. 69. Kensington Publishing Corporation, 1969.

Gilpin, Laura. *The Rio Grande.* Duell, Sloan & Pearce, Inc, 1949.

Giraudoux, Jean. French satirist playwright. *The Madwoman of Chaillot.* 1943.

Grahame, Kenneth. *The Wind in the Willows.* Methuen, 8 October, 1908. Pg. 6, 12.

Graves, John. *Goodbye to a River.* Random House Inc, 2002.

Goldstein, Vicki Nichols. From an interview between Matt Moseley and Vicki Nichols Goldstein. Vicki Nichols Goldstein is the Founder and Executive Director of the Inland Ocean Coalition. This is a conservation nonprofit dedicated to addressing the threats facing our oceans, giving those who live in inland states a voice, empowering them to take action.

Gorbachev, Mikhail. Final leader of the Soviet Union. Speech given at the 6th World Water Forum, 2012.

Haig-Brown, Roderick. *A River Never Sleeps.* Skyhorse, 1946.

Hall, Sharlot. "Song of the Colorado." From *Cactus and Pine: Songs of the Southwest.* Sherman, French & Company, 1910.

Hammerstein, Oscar. "Ol' Man River," *Showboat*, Broadway, 1927.

Handy, W.C. "Joe Turner Blues." Pace and Handy Music Co, 1915.

Hanh, Thich Nhat. *The Heart of the Buddha's Teaching: Transforming Suffering Into Peace, Joy, and Liberation.* Harmony/Rodale/Convergent, 2015.

Harvey, Paul. "So God Made a Farmer." Speech given at the 1978 Future Farmers of America Convention. The speech was first published in 1986 in Harvey's syndicated column.

Heart, Manuel. Found in Outcalt, Chris. "The Ute Mountain Ute can't access their Colorado River water rights. Here's how the tribal chairman is trying to change that." *The Colorado Sun,* 2022.

Heart, Manuel. Found in Rubin, Benjamin. "Chairman Manuel Heart looks to a new generation after five terms for the Ute Mountain Ute Tribe." *Durango Herald,* 2025.

Heller, Peter. *The Dog Stars.* Alfred A. Knopf, 2012. Pg. 56

Hemingway, Ernest, *Holiday Magazine, "The Great Blue River" 1949.* Several years before publishing *Old Man and the Sea.*

Hepburn, Audrey. "Water is life, and clean water means health." UNICEF, Facebook, April 20, 2025.

Hermingway, Ernest. *A Moveable Feast.* Scribner's, 1964.

Hesse, Hermann. *Siddhartha.* S. Fischer Verlag, 1922.

Hillman, Annelia & Gensaw, Sammy. Found in Anderson, Shane. *Guardians of the River.* American Rivers, 2022.

Hobbs, Greg. *Colorado Mother of Rivers.* Colorado Foundation for Water Education, 2005.

Hogan, Linda. "Stories of Water." From *Dwellings: A Spiritual History of the Living World.* W. W. Norton & Company, 2007.

Holmes, Oliver Wendell. Chief Justice of the Supreme Court. Case: New Jersey v. New York, etc. al., 238 U.S. 342. 1931.

The Holy Bible, King James Version. Thomas Nelson, 2017. John 7:37-38.

Holyday, Barten. 17th-century English author and clergyman. "On the River." 1631.

Hopkins, Gerard Manley. "Inversnaid." 1881.

Hough, Emerson. *The Mississippi Bubble.* Bowen-Merrill Company, 1902.

Hughes, Langston. "The Negro Speaks of Rivers." First published in *The Crisis* magazine, June 1921.

Huie, Jonathan Lockwood. Known as the 'Philosopher of Happiness.' *Quotes for Joyful Living from Daily Inspiration - Daily Quote.* Independently Published, 2011.

Isles, Alan F. and Pearn, John H. "Swimming and Survival: Two Lessons from History." *International Journal of Aquatic Research and Education: Vol. 7: No. 2, Article 8.* 2013.

Johnson, Lyndon B. "Special Message to the Congress on Conservation and Restoration of Natural Beauty." LBJ Presidential Library, 1965.

Jung, C.G. *Collected Works of C.G Jung.* Translated by R.F.C. Hull. Princeton: Princeton University Press. 1972.

Kabat-Zan, Jon. *Full Catastrophe Living.* Random House, 1990.

Kabotie, Ed, Hopi musician, Facebook post, March 30, 2019.

Kahanamoku, Duke. Famous Hawaiian who popularized surfing. This quote is engraved under his statue at Waikiki Beach.

Kalwar, Santosh. *Quote Me Everyday.* Lulu, 2010.

Kauffman, John. *Flow East: A Look at Our North Atlantic Rivers.* McGraw-Hill, 1973.

Kellerman, Annette. Quoted by her, in the book: Means, Howard. *Splash! 10,000 Years of Swimming.* Grand Central Publishing, June 2, 2020.

Kemmis, Dan. "Community and the Politics of Place." *Harper's Magazine.* February 1991.

Khan, Sanober. *A Thousand Flamingos.* Cyberwit, 2020.

Kiernan, Tom. "Statement from Our President and CEO, Tom Kiernan." American Rivers, YouTube. Jan 30, 2025.

Kipling, Rudyard. "The Prairie." From *The Seven Seas.* D. Appleton & Company, 1896.

Kitzhaber, John. Former governor of Oregon. "A Tale of Two Rivers: National Conference of Trout Unlimited." August 16, 2000.

Kimmerer, Robin Wall. *Braiding Sweetgrass.* Milkweed Editions, 2013. Pg. 55.

Kuralt, Charles. *On the Road with Charles Kuralt.* A CBS Evening News show that ran from 1967 to 1980, in which Kuralt traveled the country in a motor home and told the stories of ordinary people.

Lakota Prophesy. Encapsulates the fundamental belief in water's essential role for survival and well-being.

Larcom, Lucy. *The Unseen friend.* The Riverside Press, 1892.

Lawrence, D. H. *Pansies.* 1926.

Lee, Katie. (October 23, 1919 – November 1, 2017) was an American folk singer, actress, writer, photographer and environmental activist. From the 1950s, Lee often sang about rivers and white water rafting. She was a vocal opponent of Glen Canyon Dam, which closed its gates in 1963, and called for the canyon to be returned to its natural state. For her environmental activism, she was often called "the Desert Goddess of Glen Canyon." Her obituary in The New York Times states, "Ms. Lee never forgave the builders of the Glen Canyon Dam and said the only thing that prevented her from blowing it up was that she did not know how."

Lee, Bruce Silliphant, Stirling & Rogosin, Joel. *Longstreet* (TV Series). ABC, 1971-72.

Leitch, Mary Stinton. "The River." From *The Waggon and the Star.* B.J. Brimmer, 1922.

Leopold, Aldo. *A Sand County Almanac.* Oxford University Press, 1949. Pg. 34, 124, 163.

Leopold, Luna. USGS. "Lessons Learned from a Legend: Luna Leopold." United States Geological Survey, 2015.

Lermontov, Mikhail. *A Hero of Our Time.* Iliya Glazunov & Co, 1840 Pg. 126.

Longfellow, Henry Wadsworth. "The Secret of the Sea." From *The Seaside and the Fireside.* Public domain, 1850.

Lopez, Barry. "Drought." *Northwest Journal of Law & Policy*, 1994.

Lord Byron, "Child Harold's Pilgrimage." *Canto III.* 1812.

Lord Byron, "It is the Hour." *Hebrew Melodies.* 1815.

Lord Byron. *Don Juan* Canto II, Stanza 84. Hudson Street Press, 1918.

Lord Byron, Letter to his friend and publisher, John Murray, dated August 12, 1821, written from Ravenna, Italy, describing his daily routine and love for swimming.

Lord Swinburne, Philbrick, Nathaniel. *In the Heart of the Sea: The Tragedy of the Whaleship Essex.* Viking Press, 2000.

Lubbock, Sir John. *The Use of Life.* Macmillan & co, 1894.

Macfarlane, Robert. *Is a River Alive?*. Pg. 15. W. W. Norton & Company, May 20, 2025.

Maclean, Norman. *A River Runs Through It.* University of Chicago Press, May 1976. Pg. 158.

Martin, George R. R. Lord Varies. *A Clash of Kings.* Bantam Spectra, 1999.

Matos Ortiz, Joel. "Son of Water." Ortiz is a Guiness World Record Swimmer from San Juan, Puerto Rico.

Malloch, Douglas. "Uncle Sam's River." A. H. Stockwell, 1928.

Maltby, Edward. *Waterlogged Wealth.* Agribookstore, 1986.

Marks, William. *The Holy Order of Water: Healing the Earth's Waters and Ourselves.* Bell Pond Books, 2001.

Marryat, Friedrick (Captain). *A Diary in America.* D. Appleton & Co, 1839.

Marshall, Bob. "The Wilderness as a Minority Right." From *The Living Wilderness* magazine, 1933.

McBride, Peter. *Silent River.* American Rivers, 2022.

McBride, Peter. "The latest word from our rivers: we all need to use less." *Instagram.* August 19, 2025.

McCully, Patrick. *Silenced Rivers.* Bloomsbury Academic, 1996.

McGhee, Alison. *All Rivers Flow to the Sea.* Candlewick, 2005.

McGuane, Tom & Barbato, Joseph, et. al. *Heart of the Land: Essays on the Last Great Places.* Knopf Doubleday Publishing Group, 1996.

Means, Howard. *Splash! 10,000 Years of Swimming.* Grand Central Publishing, June 2, 2020.

Melville, Herman. *Moby Dick.* Harper & Brothers, 1851.

Merriman, H. S. *The Sowers.* Harper & Brothers, 1895.

"Message from Hopi Elders." Angelfire, 2001.

Michener, James A. *Centennial* Random House, 1974. Pg. 888. Paul Garrett on a flyover of the Platte river while missing a University of Colorado football game.

Middleton, Harry. *Rivers of Memory.* Westwinds Press, 1993.

Milne, A. A. *Winnie the Pooh.* Dutton, 1926.

Milne, A. A. *A. A. Milne's Winnie-the-Pooh*, specifically from chapter 10 of the original 1926 book, *Winnie-the-Pooh and Piglet Build a House.*

Miniuk, Colleen. *Current Flows* Exhibit, Santa Fe, NM. 2001.

Miniuk, Colleen. *So Said the River: Life, Loss, and Pie on the Colorado.* Analemma Press, 2024.

Mitchell, Becky & et al. "Voices: We represent the Upper Basin states, and it's time we manage the Colorado River we have — not the one we want." *The Salt Lake Tribune*, Dec. 6, 2024.

Mni Wiconi: Water is Life. A Lakota term encapsulating water's essential role for survival and wellbeing. This term was used as a protest slogan, during the Standing Rock Protests, against the construction of the Dakota Access Pipeline. A good resource about the saying and its significance to the Lakota and Sioux tribes as a whole: https://www.culturalsurvival.org/publications/cultural-survival-quarterly/water-life-rise-mni-wiconi-movement

Momaday, N. Scott. *Earth Keeper: Reflections on the American Land.* Harper, 2020.

Moore, Kathleen Dean & Moore, Jonathan W. "The Gift of Salmon." *Discover Magazine.* May, 2003.

Moore, Thomas. *The Re-Enchantment of Everyday Life.* Harper Perennial, May 14, 1996.

Morley, Christopher. *The Romany Stain.* Doubleday, Page & Co., 1926.

Moseley, Matthew L. *Soul is Waterproof.* CG Sports Publishing, 2023.

Muir, John. "Mountain Thoughts." From *John of the Mountains.* Sierra Club, 1938.

Munatones, Steven. *Open Water Swimming: Improved Performance for Swimmers and Triathletes.* Human Kinetics, June 14, 2011.

Muskie, Ed. Senator Muskie (Maine) argued for the passage of the Clean Water Act in 1972, CRS, 1972 Legislative History P164, 161-162.

Naskar, Abhijit. *Citizens of Peace: Beyond the Savagery of Sovereignty.* Independently Published, 2019.

National Geographic Special Edition: *Water: The Power, Promise, and Turmoil of North America's Fresh Water.* 1993.

Dr. Necefer, Len. "The Dry Colorado River: A Cross-Border Gravel Bike Journey with Len Necefer." Outside TV, 2025. Dr. Necefer is also quoted in the documentary, *What the River Knows*. Necefer, Ph.D. is the CEO & Founder of NativesOutdoors – a native owned outdoor media, apparel and consulting company. He is also a filmmaker and Indigenous activist. He is a member of the Navajo tribe.

Neruda, Pablo, *All the Odes*, edited by Ilan Stavans, Farrar Straus Giroux, New York. 1973.

Nichols, John. *The Milagro Beanfield War*. Random House Press, 1974.

Nichols, Wallace J. *Blue Mind: The Surprising Science That Shows How Being Near, In, On, Or Under Water Can Make You Happier, Healthier, More Connected, and Better at What You Do.* Little, Brown and Company, July 22, 2014.

Nietzsche, Friedrich. *Ecce Homo.* Penguin Classics, 1908.

Noel, Lynn. *Voyages: Canada's Heritage Rivers.* Breakwater Books, 1995.

Norse, Elliott. *Global Marine Biological Diversity: A Strategy For Building Conservation Into Decision Making.* Island Press, 1993.

Ondaatje, Michael. *The English Patient*. McClelland & Stewart. September 1992.

O'Donohue, John. "Fluent" from *Conamara Blues.* Perennial Publishing, January 16, 2004.

O'Konski, Alvin. Wisconsin congressman about the St. Croix River. O'Konski was one of the major advocates of the Wild and Scenic Rivers Act, which now protects the St. Croix river.

Oliver, Mary. *White Pine.* Harcourt Brace, 1996.

Olson, Larry & Daniel, John. *Oregon Rivers.* Westcliffe Publishers, 1997.

Olson, Sigurd. *The Singing Wilderness.* Knopf Doubleday Publishing, 1956.

Olson, Sigurd. *Open Horizons.* University of Minnesota Press, 1969.

Ovid & Simpson, Michael (translator). *The Metamorphoses of Ovid.* University of Massachusetts, 2001.

Palmer, Tim. *The Wild and Scenic Rivers of America.* Island Press, 1993.

Palmer, Tim. *Lifelines: The Case for River Conservation.* Rowman & Littlefield Publishers, 2004.

Perls, Fritz. *Gesalt Therapy Verbatim.* Real People Press, 1969.

Phelps, Michael. Donald McRae. "Interview Michael Phelps." The Guardian, 2004.

Pindar & Race, William H. *Olympian Odes. Pythian Odes.* Harvard University Press, 1997.

Pinkola Estes, Clarissa, Ph.D. *Women Who Run With the Wolves: Myths and Stories of the Wild Woman Archetype.* Chapter 10, pg. 323.

Plato. *Laws, Book 3*, Section 689d.

Plautus, Titus Maccius. *Poenulus, or The Little Carthaginian.* 190 BC. Act 3, Scene 3, Line 14.

Poe, Edgar Allan. "To the River." From *Al Aaraaf, Tamerlane, and Minor Poems*, Hatch and Dunning, 1929.

Popov, Alexandr. Said during the 1992 Barcelona Olympics.

Porter, Eliot. *The Place No One Knew.* Sierra Club, 1963. Pg. 18.

Postel, Sandra. *Last Oasis: Facing Water Scarcity.* W. W. Norton & Co, June 17, 1997. Pg. 184.

Powell, John Wesley. *The Exploration of the Colorado River and its Canyons.* Penguin Random House, 1895.

Quamman, David. *Grabbing the Loop.* Scribner, 2012.

Ramakrishna, Sri & Gupta, Mahendranath. *The Gospel of Sri Ramakrishna.* Ramakrishna-Vivekananda Center, 1902.

Ramos, Sullen, Povo Indígena Goyá, Brazil. As told to author on January 15, 2026.

Rawlings, Marjorie Kinnan. *Cross Creek.* C. Scribner's Sons, 1942.

Reilly, John C., Source unknown.

Reisner, Marc. *Cadillac Desert: The American West and Its Disappearing Water.* Viking Press, 1986.

Rennicke, Jeff. *River Days: Travels on Western Rivers.* Fulcrum, 1988.

Rilke, Rainer Maria. *Rilke's Book of Hours: Love Poems to God.* Insel-Verlag, 1905.

Robbins, Tom. *Fierce Invalids from Hot Climates.* Bantam, 2000.

Roberts, Elizabeth. *Earth Prayers: 365 Prayers, Poems, and Invocations for Honoring the Earth.* Harper Collins, 1991.

Robinson, Edwin Arlington. *Roman Bartholow.* Macmillan, 1923.

Roosevelt, Theodore. "Our Vanishing Wildlife," State of the Union Address, 1908.

Rumi. He was a poet and theologian born in the 13th century, considered one of the greatest poets in the Persian language.

Rumi & Barks, Coleman. *The Essential Rumi.* Castle Books, 1995.

Russell, Andy. *The Life of a River.* McClelland & Stewart, 1987.

Sacks, Oliver. "Water Babies." *The New Yorker*. May 19, 1997.

Sáenz, Benjamin Alire, *Aristotle and Dante Discover the Secrets of the Universe.* Simon & Schuster, 2012.

Sagan, Carl. *Pale Blue Dot: A Vision of the Human Future in Space.* Random House, 1994.

Schieffer, Shane. *The Tao of a River Guide*. Schieffer is a friend of Moseley and open water swimmer who swam the entire length of Lake Powell solo towing his own equipment in 2025.

Serageldin, Ismail (PhD). "Wars of the Twenty-First Century," World Bank Press Conference, 1995.

Shakespeare, William. *A Midsummer Night's Dream.* Royal Shakespeare Company, 1600.

Shakespeare, William. *The Tempest.* Royal Shakespeare Company, 1611.

Shakespeare, William. *As You Like It.* Royal Shakespeare Company, 1623.

Shakespeare, William. *Hamlet.* Royal Shakespeare Company, 1623.

Shelley, Percy Bysshe. "The Cloud." C. & J. Ollier, 1820.

Shozo, Tanako. He was a politician and social activist in Japan who lived from 1841 to 1913. He advocated for the rural residents around the Watarase River, which was downstream from a copper mine and poisoning those who lived close to the river. He ended up risking his own imprisonment/life when he delivered a petition directly to the Japanese emperor by intercepting his carriage.

Sophocles & Stavropoulos, Steven. *The Beginning of All Wisdom.* Pg. 106. Marlowe & Company, 2003.

Southey, Robert. "The Cataract of Lodore." 1820. This poem is about Lodore Falls in England. This poem is the namesake for the Gates of Lodore on the Green River in Dinosaur National Monument.

Sparks, Nicholas. *The Notebook.* Warner Books, 1996.

Stegner, Wallace. *The Sound of Mountain Water: The Changing American West.* Penguin Random House, 1969.

Stevenson, Robert Louis. "Where Go the Boats?" *A Child's Garden of Verses and Underwoods.* Longmans, Green, & Co, 1885.

Strings, Billy. @billystrings. "Happy Earth Day People." *Instagram.* April 22, 2021.

Szent-Györgyi, Albert. "Biology and Pathology of Water." *Perspectives in Biology and Medicine, vol. 14 no. 2*, p. 239-249. Project MUSE, 1971.

Tagore, Rabindranath. *Stray Birds*. A & D Books, 1916.

Teale, Edwin Way. *Journey Into Summer A Naturalist's Record of a 19,000 Mile Journey through the North American Summer.* Dodd, Mead & Company, 1960.

Tennyson, Lord Alfred. "The Brook." From *Maud, and Other Poems.* Edward Moxon, 1855.

Thien-An, Thich. *Zen Philosophy, Zen Practice.* Dharma Publishing, 1975. Pg. 118.

Thomas, Sarah. First person to swim the English Channel four times consecutively. From a personal interview with Moseley, 2023.

Thoreau, Henry David. *The Journal of Henry David Thoreau, 1837-1861*. NYRB Classics, 2009.

Thoreau, Henry David. *A Week on the Concord and Merrimack Rivers.* Self-Published, 1849.

Thoreau, Henry David. *Walden; or Life in the Woods.* Ticknor and Fields, 1854. Pg. 247.

Thoreau, Henry David. *The Main Woods*. Ticknor and Fields, 1864.

Thoreau, Henry David. *Cape Cod*. Ticknor and Fields, 1866.

Thorson, John. Water rights lawyer and co-founder of the organization "Dividing the Waters."

Tolkien, J.R.R. *The Silmarillion.* George Allen & Unwin, 1977.

Tsui, Bonnie. *Why We Swim.* Algonquin Books, 2020.

Twain, Mark. "Letter to William Bowen," 1867.

Twain, Mark. "Two Ways of Seeing A River" *Life on the Mississippi*. Pg. 112. Signet Classics, 1883.

Twain, Mark. *The Adventures of Huckleberry Finn.* Charles L. Webster And Company, 1885.

Tzu, Lao and Mitchell, Stephen. *Tao Te Ching: A New English Version.* (*Tao Te Ching,* 4th-6th Century BC). Chapter 78. Harper Collins, 1988.

US Department of the Interior. *River of Life, Water: the Environmental Challenge.* U.S. Government Printing Office, 1970.

Van Dyke, Henry. *Little Rivers: A Book of Essays in Profitable Idleness.* Charles Scribner's Sons, 1895.

Vigil, Daryl & Peterson, Brittany & Outcalt, Chris. "100 years after compact, Colorado River nearing crisis point." *Public Broadcasting Service.* Sep 12, 2022.

Virgil, Roman Poet. *Georgics.* 29 BC.

Vold, Jan Erik. Norwegian Poet. "What All the World Knows (Det Alle Vet)." 1970.

Voltaire. *A Philosophical Dictionary* Vol. 1, Pg. 139. Gabriel Grasset, 1764.

Warner, Edith. *In the Shadows of Los Alamos: Selected Writings of Edith Warner.* UNM Press, 2008.

Waters, Frank. "The Place No One Knew." *Sierra Club Bulletin.* December, 1965.

Wallace, David Foster. "This is Water," commencement speech at Kenyon College, 2005.

Wallach, Jeff. *What the River Says: Whitewater Journeys Along the Inner Frontier.* Blue Heron Publishing, 1996.

Whitman, Walt. "Of the Waters." *Leaves of Grass,* 1855.

Whitman, Walt. "The Sleepers." *Leaves of Grass,* 1855.

Whitman, Walt. *Passage to India,* 1871.

Wilkinson, Charles & Marston, Ed. "Charles Wilkinson crows over the corpse of the West's traditional approach to water." *High Country News*, August 12, 1991.

Williams, Terry Tempest. *The Open Space of Democracy*. Wipf & Stock Publishers, 2009.

Williams, Terry Tempest. *When Women Were Birds*. Picador, February 26, 2013. Pg. 20, 169.

Williams, Terry Tempest & Kupfer, David. "Terry Tempest Williams Interview." *The Progressive Magazine*. February 1, 2005.

Wilson, Woodrow. *The New Freedom,* collection of speeches from 1912 presidential campaign.

Wright, Jim. *The Coming Water Famine.* Coward-McCann, 1966.

Wolfe, Thomas. *Of Time and the River.* Charles Scribner's Sons, 1935.

Wordsworth, William. *Guide to the Lakes.* Kendall Hudson & Nicholson, 1810.

Wordsworth, William. *The River Duddon : a series of sonnets.* Longman, Hurst, Rees, Orme, and Brown, 1820.

Wroblewski, David. *The Story of Edgar Sawtelle*. Harper Collins, 2008.

Yanagihara, Hanna, *A Brisk Swim Across Martha's Vineyard, New York Times,* February, 4, 2016.

YatraDham, on the Kumbh Mela. The Kumbh Mela is the largest celebration of water on the planet. It is a powerful symbol of faith and unity, and many quotes reflect its significance. Some highlight the spiritual cleansing of the sacred waters, while others emphasize the transformative powers and the feeling of unity it fosters.

# Sources

# Index of Quote Sources